"Funny, witty, gritty, and deeply shocking! *With An Early Adolescence*, Fisher vividly shares his cultural crucibles while growing up in Thailand during the early 1970s. He portrays his military family, friends, and the people of Thailand with so much authenticity you feel as if you are right beside him . . . through his fantastical cultural delights, sumptuous temptations, moral dilemmas, and terrifying dangers. Autobiographical storytelling doesn't get any better than this. You will laugh and you will cry. It is a fast roller coaster of a ride. Hang on tight."

—**Lieutenant Colonel Scott A. Porter (USA, Ret.)**, Author of *Here They Come*, American Fiction Awards Winner

"Mike Fisher's *An Early Adolescence* is much more than a memoir. Fisher uses the unique travels and characters of his earlier years as a laboratory to investigate the quest for belonging, identity, and self that each of us endures, both in childhood and through our adult years. His writing is clear, precise, and accessible, his story is memorable, and his themes are universal and timeless. Mike Fisher explains his childhood and in so doing shows us all a bit about ourselves."

—**Greg Fields**, Author of *Through the Waters and the Wild*, 2022 Independent Press Award Winner, Literary Fiction

"Fisher's is a fascinating memoir of growing up as an Army brat in Bangkok, Thailand, during the waning years of the Vietnam War. Against the backdrop of your typical American boyhood—elementary school, Boy Scouts, and Little League—Fisher's tales are anything but typical. Rather, his is a boy's adventure story set in an exotic culture where your maid has no qualms about hiring a hitman to take out a competitor. You'll have to buy the book to discover if she gets away with it."

—**Michael Little**, The Daily Vinyl

An Early Adolescence

by Michael Fisher

ISBN 978-1-64663-917-5

Published by

 köehlerbooks™

3705 Shore Drive
Virginia Beach, VA 23455
800-435-4811
www.koehlerbooks.com

AN EARLY
ADOLESCENCE

AN AMERICAN BOY GROWS UP IN THE
THAI KINGDOM OF RAMA THE 9TH

MICHAEL P. FISHER

VIRGINIA BEACH
CAPE CHARLES

TABLE OF CONTENTS

FOREWORD

The time sandwiched between 1972 and 1975 was, for me, full of the middle-class uneventfulness that characterized growing up in a suburban Southern neighborhood. At eight years old in 1972, I was just beginning to individuate from my parents' taste in music, most notably Ferrante & Teicher and Arthur Fiedler and the Boston Pops, to Elton John and Electric Light Orchestra. I had a pair of white go-go boots to go along with my dreams of the many big things I would do. I watched the Atlanta Braves play ball with my mom, and football with my dad. I often annoyed my older brother. I walked to the neighborhood grocery to buy a Coke and Little Debbie snack cakes and, later, to look and giggle at the cute boys who stocked shelves and bagged groceries. All very routine, safe, and expected.

This book, however, is not about routine, safe, and expected.

When I met Michael Fisher, my husband, in the summer of 2014, I spent much of my time wide eyed and open mouthed in surprise at what he had seen and experienced as a child in Bangkok, then as a teen in Belgium, a young Army officer in the Gulf War, and later while experiencing an illness that ended his military career. I realized early on that adapting to change was not just a way of life for him but also a strength born out of unusual life circumstances and geography. But more than just adapting to change, I saw immediately in Michael his ability to completely live in each moment of life.

We often speak of living life to its fullest and that it is usually a skill learned after living for some time on this earth, or perhaps after surviving some significant illness or accident. Mike learned it before he even hit puberty. The stories in this book explain how a young boy from North Carolina obtained such an appreciation for life and the moments in it. Fortunately, having a well-developed memory for detail is a strength for Michael. His experiences come alive in this book because of these remembered details, as well as his unaffected and unique perspective.

Cheryl Fisher

PREFACE

The 1960s were not kind to my mother. She became pregnant with me her first year at East Carolina, then married the guy who did it to her, my biological father. The biological part was his only contribution. He turned out to be emotionally and physically abusive and was also into drugs, booze, and extracurricular sexual activities. So as the short marriage fell apart, he split to live the life of a 1960s love child in California, never supporting Mom or my brother and me. Nothing. Mom wisely took steps to end the marriage and, having no choice, moved us in with her parents in Fayetteville, North Carolina.

Things got worse when my grandfather died a couple years later, leaving the care of my brother and me to Mom and my grandmother. They both managed incredible feats to keep things afloat, but these were meager times.

Everything changed in 1971 when my mom met a young Army officer, the man I consider my true father. Within a year of our meeting, Mom and Dad married and we found ourselves moving to the other side of the globe, to Bangkok, Thailand.

Many things changed in our lives, far more than just the environment. It was a dangerous time in Southeast Asia. The war in Vietnam was ending, and Thailand feared it would be the next country in a series of communist-led invasions. There was similar political turmoil within the country, and life in such a large and bustling city was both magical and dangerous.

But this is a story about the beginnings of a new family, and a kid that went from being very poor, losing all the male father figures

5

in his life, to one of privilege and adventure in a foreign country. The book discusses family, culture, and race from a different perspective, and the stories are unique and surprising. There's no way you can guess what's inside.

I could not have written this book without the help of my wife, Cheryl. She has been the voice of reason, compassion, and love in my life. It makes sense that she played the same role in the creation of this work.

Thanks also to all my friends with whom I have shared the book, for your open and honest opinion. Your honesty has made me learn from my mistakes. A true friend is one who has that type of courage.

I want to thank my mother. We lost her in 2018. The second bout with cancer devoured her, and after, Dad and I went through a tough period. I am not sure it was his fear of losing his place as the family patriarch, or just blind grief. But we all learned Mom was the strength and stabilizing factor in our lives. It takes an angel and a strong person to be the calming influence in a house of childish and self-centered men.

Lastly, I must thank my father. All of this was because of him. Dad saved us. He took us from a life of near poverty with little hope of a real future other than joining the Army and gave us the world. I am the man I have become because of the love, guidance, and opportunity he provided. Thank you. I love you.

CHAPTER 1

Fayetteville, North Carolina, Summer 1971

I will never forget the day we met him.

Our grandmother, Amma, had me and my brother out in the summer heat, mowing the lawn of our post-war bungalow. I never understood why mowing in hundred-degree temperatures was mandatory. What mostly grew in the Piedmont region of North Carolina during the heat of the year were sour weeds and sand spurs. Centipede grass constantly battled with crabgrass for supremacy, hastily covering the ground and creeping across the yard rather than growing vertically. The stuff was as tough as Texas, but the sand beneath it was winning the battle. The lawnmower only managed to create great dust clouds that covered everything. Amma's constant gaze kept us soldiering on. She was a tough country girl and would never hesitate to cut a switch from a nearby bush and tan our asses if we slacked off.

All of a sudden, a new burgundy Corvette pulled up to the house—a Stingray, one with the big engine that roared when a driver would "stand on it." It was shiny with a T-top, black interior, spoke wheels. How cool! Then the driver got out, dressed in starched Army fatigues, spit-shined paratrooper boots, and Ray-Ban shooters across his unseen eyes. He was one of those "soldier fellers" from Fort Bragg. All activity in the yard stopped.

Amma remained seated on the front porch, smoking a Herbert Tareyton cigarette and barking orders at us. "You missed a spot over there, boys. Then get to the side of the house. If you're thirsty, have a drink from the hosepipe. I need to get started with supper."

"Okay, Amma! What's for supper?" Mark asked.

"Fried chicken, squash, stewed okra, and sliced tomatoes," she replied.

"Squash? I hate squash, and she always makes sit me there until I eat it all," I whispered to Mark.

"I heard that, boy. Get your ass to work!"

The Corvette driver finally spoke up. "Hi. I'm Paul Fisher. I'm here to get Page."

Amma replied with her cigarette in her mouth. "I've heard of you. Let me go get her. This child is going to be thirty minutes late for her own damn funeral."

As Amma left, Paul turned his attention to me and Mark. We stood quiet, waiting for him to speak. "Who are you guys?" he asked.

"I'm Mike, and this is my brother, Mark."

"Hey!" Mark threw in.

"I'm kidding. I know who you are. Your mom can't stop talking about you. You guys are working pretty hard. I'm impressed. It's really good that you work around the house, help your mom and grandmother. Where do you guys go to school? What do you like to do?"

"Ramsey Street School," Mark said. "I hate it."

"I don't hate it that much," I replied. "I also play baseball at Tokay Little League. I'm a catcher, like my granddaddy."

"I was really sorry to hear about your granddaddy. Your mother truly loved him, and he loved all of you. I wish I could have met him. I'm sure I would have liked him. Anyway, I really like your mom. I hope it's okay for me to see her."

Mark and I nodded in agreement.

Mom appeared on the porch, perfectly quaffed, beautiful as always. Everyone's attention moved to her. Her brunette hair was teased to perfection; she had a deep-brown tan and wore a fashionable outfit for the period. How could you not be engrossed by her presence? We could tell that Paul felt more for her than just simple attraction. He took her by the hand.

"Nice to meet you, Ms. Beasley . . . boys," Paul said. "I hope to see you soon."

"Nice to meet you, too," Amma replied. "Boys, time to get ready for supper. Go to the bathroom and get cleaned up. We'll finish the yard tomorrow."

"You boys be good. Hear me?" Mom said as she moved toward the car.

"Yes ma'am!" we shouted.

Paul held the door for her, and she slipped in the shiny rocket car. Paul raced to the other side, hopped in, and gave Mom a quick kiss. The engine roared and they sped off.

Mark and I stood and watched in awe.

Mom had moved us in with Amma and Granddaddy after the failure of her marriage in '67 to our biological father. She worked full-time, and Amma ran the household. Granddaddy passed away in 1970. He was our hero, and it shook our foundation. So, to see a man, a potential stepfather, in the yard meant much more than having a random stranger appear. There was something about him, his presence, his stature, and we felt it. Mark and I had been fatherless since Mom's divorce and Granddaddy's death. Our biological father had gotten caught up in the 1960s free-love, drugs, and rock 'n roll movement, and was last known to be somewhere on the West Coast.

We were now townies, living a life separate from sometimes rival factions in town. Neatly quaffed men wore short-sleeve button-down shirts over trousers and loafers or business suits around Hay Street and the Market House. Women dressed up to go downtown, sporting big hairdos that resembled football helmets. They carried pocketbooks that looked large enough to hold a week's food supply. Church was the social event of the week. Holiday parades included the band from Terry Sanford High and the Shriner's go-kart troop.

We lived among the remnants of the Old South, and the civil rights movement had finally come to town. During my first year at Lucille Souders Elementary, there was not a "colored" face in the class. And I hated that term. Didn't we all have a "color"?

The next year we were bussed downtown to Ramsey Street Elementary for the new normal. I remember Amma and Granddaddy being upset over the change, but the reality in the classroom helped placate worries. Initially, we sat on opposite sides of the class—segregated. But eventually, eyes began to make contact, smiles began to appear, and soon the playground was blended. I still remember the little girl who sat next to me. I couldn't look at her at first—not because she was Black but because I was terribly shy and terrified of girls. Every time I would peek at her, she would look at me with piercing brown eyes, and a beautiful wide smile. I wonder why I remember her. I guess she was my first crush.

We lived in a simple home, three small bedrooms, a bath, and, common in the South, an eat-in kitchen. The neighborhood was in a state of decline. Our neighborhood was once a respectable middle-class area, but many families nearby were buying new split-level brick homes on the outskirts of the city. Others were sadly losing their breadwinners, so nice family houses were falling into a state of slow decay. The men who returned home from the Second World War and built the neighborhood were now in their sixties, looking forward to retirement, or dying. Some were just attempting to escape desegregation.

In the late '60s, a new group who changed things appeared in town. Earlier in the decade, downtown was pristine and vibrant. I remember Granddaddy taking me to get a haircut on Hay Street and then to lunch at the Haymont Grill. The counterculture had descended upon us. Hippies, drug dealers, and prostitutes began to take hold in the establishments on Hay Street that, just a year earlier, were a proud part of the economic and social environment. In our neighborhood, a motorcycle gang moved into the house two doors down.

Crime and urban decay became the issue of the day, and it catered to everyone, especially young soldiers from Fort Bragg. The war in Vietnam was still raging, and of course Fayetteville and Fort Bragg did their part to feed troops to the war. But the counterculture in town was more than a player in the national fever to end the war; it fed the dark side. Soldiers returning home with drug habits, or those who joined the Army already addicted, found nurture in the new seedy areas of town.

It took decades to remedy the issue. In the 1990s, Fayetteville built a new police department headquarters in the heart of Hay Street, and slowly businesses began to return and attract people. The first mall in the area was built during the same time, dragging most financial activity away from downtown to the Cross Creek area of town. The Fayetteville I remembered as a little boy was gone. Today, Hay Street is safe, but economic resurgence has been lethargic.

You can't talk about Fayetteville and not discuss Fort Bragg. Now one of the nation's largest military posts, it pumps billions of dollars into the local economy every year, but it has done its part in stripping Fayetteville of its identity as a charming Southern town. At the beginning of the Second World War, the War Department was looking for places to build training posts to meet the demand for soldiers. Always looking for the best deal possible, Fayetteville was chosen because it basically had no economy. Land was cheap, really cheap. Some crops grew in the sand hills, but not enough to move the area out of the lingering effects of the Great Depression. So, thousands of acres were purchased by the federal government, encampments were built to house soldiers, businesses supporting soldiers and their families began popping up, and, boom, Fayetteville was thriving. What made it exciting was that Fort Bragg was full of paratroopers, which meant we lived next to 50,000 people who all could be certified as batshit crazy. When you think about it, Fayetteville is an extremely lucky place. There will always be a thriving economy because of the Army post.

When attending North Carolina State in the early 1980s, my fraternity brothers would kid me, saying Fayetteville is not North Carolina because of Fort Bragg. When visiting small towns around the state, I realized maybe they were right. So much of North Carolina was truly Mayberry of *Andy Griffith Show* fame, based on his hometown of Mount Airy. By comparison, Fayetteville was like living inside a roller derby match.

Although my grandparents were originally from Virginia, when settling in Fayetteville permanently after the war they considered themselves locals and, more importantly, North Carolinians. Granddaddy was a city boy from Richmond, and Amma grew up on a tobacco farm in south-central Virginia. When her parents died, her brothers and sisters were given equal portions of the family farm. Amma immediately sold her share to her brother Leroy, then took her winnings to Richmond and the good life. During her party-girl period, she was crowned Miss Buckroe Beach, Virginia. Thankfully, after running out of money and being relegated back to working class, she met Granddaddy. She was a small woman with a petite frame. She wore Dame Edna glasses that no one on the planet found attractive, and she smoked cigarettes. Her education ended in the seventh grade, so she lived her life in Fayetteville as a housewife and mother.

When Granddaddy died, Amma's life went from a comfortable middle-class existence to having to figure out how to earn a living. Granddaddy had been an insurance salesman, but he didn't leave Amma or Mom a life insurance policy, or any sort of inheritance. To make matters worse, Granddaddy died just months before his own retirement, and for some reason—and this still does not sound right to me—his company gave nothing to Amma financially. The only thing she got, after her husband's thirty years of service to this company, was a diamond-encrusted pin. I remember a photo of her with the two heads of this company, tears streaming down her face. She was left destitute. Years later, I asked her why she never hired an attorney to fight this situation, but her lack of education and sophistication hindered her.

Still, Amma made things happen. She had a large garden in the backyard, but sewing was her forte. She was an amazing seamstress. Women would come to the house to have dresses personally tailored. She would make custom drapery for homes. But still, with all her hard work, times were meager. Mom worked full-time, and Amma made do, but my brother, Mark, and I had little. I remember only owning two shirts and two pairs of pants at one point. On cold winter mornings, Amma would make a fire in the fireplace for us, and we would huddle by each other. She would heat the opposite end of the house with the kitchen stove. Thankfully, shortly after Granddaddy died, we got notice that the mortgage was paid in full. I remember her yelling with joy in the front yard as she opened the mail.

She was, and is to this day, the best cook I have ever known. We ate like Southerners. My favorite meal was fried chicken and any vegetable combination she chose, and we ate a lot of vegetables. She was reason I love okra, butter beans, collard greens, and anything commonly found on a table in the agrarian South of the time. Her lemon cheesecake was heaven, but things like beef liver, chicken gizzards, and pig feet were among the things she liked and insisted we eat, none of which appealed to me. I was not interested in pig rooter to the tooter.

How we ate changed after Grandaddy's passing. While Amma and Mom were figuring out our new economic reality, I remember eating dumplings and gravy for days at a time. Dumplings are merely flour, salt, and water, which illustrates the dire nature of the situation. I can't eat dumplings to this day. But she and Mom saved us. Amma surely earned her place next to God.

Sadly, because she smoked heavily, she died in 1997 of complications from emphysema. Everyone smoked then, especially young girls growing up on Virginia tobacco farms.

Granddaddy was a big man, standing over six foot two. Before the war, he suffered a failed marriage. I know little of the affair, and of course, Amma never wanted to discuss it. He played catcher for minor league baseball in Richmond. This was the primary reason I took up the position when I played baseball in my younger years. Amma would say that he caught for Babe Ruth when the Great Bambino spent a short stint in the Carolina League, but the dates of this chance occurrence never added up. Granddaddy was born 1909, and Ruth played in North Carolina before 1920—in fact hitting his first major league home run in Fayetteville. Granddaddy may have been good, but not good enough at age ten to play with the Great Bambino. I realized in my adult years that Amma was just trying to motivate me to play.

During the war, Granddaddy was an Army medic stationed at Camp Mackall, a large training post adjacent to Fort Bragg. His job was to work in a clinic and give inoculations to troops passing through for training. He would joke, saying he fought the Germans by shooting them in the "tuchus" with needles. It made me laugh every time. He had an amazing sense of humor. He never deployed overseas, which allowed him and Amma to maintain a relatively normal family life during the war and, most importantly, to conceive my mother. After the war ended, they went back to Richmond for a short period but were both homesick for Fayetteville. They returned home, bought the house we were living in, and stayed.

Being that I was a little boy whose father had disappeared, Granddaddy became my hero. I still remember him chasing me around the house as I shrieked with glee. I would wake up in the morning with him, before work, and he would make eggs, grits, and toast for us and have the coffee ready for Amma.

Also, every morning he would take medications from the refrigerator and give himself a shot of insulin. All those years at Camp Mackall had to account for something, but diabetes was taking a toll on him.

He had three heart attacks before he passed. One of them was when he and I were home alone. Amma was out at a local laundry washing clothes, and Granddaddy started to have chest pain. He begged me to call her on the phone, but I was five at most and had no idea what to do. I began to panic and cry. I remember fumbling with the rotary dial phone, hoping Amma would answer. Thankfully, a moment later Amma came in the door. She called Granddaddy's best friend, a man named Cecil Butler. Cecil was quite the character—whiskey, cigars, horses, fast cars, women. He responded much faster than any ambulance. He raced to the house in his black 1968 Lincoln Continental, the kind with suicide doors, dragged Granddaddy into the back, and raced like hell to Cape Fear Valley Hospital. It saved Granddaddy's life, but he was never the same afterward. He was no longer capable of chasing me around the house. He could no longer raise his arms to shave or comb his hair. Amma did these things for him. I didn't understand that he was dying.

His third heart attack was his final. One night, Amma took me and Mark to see the Ringling Brothers Circus at the Coliseum, and suddenly over the public address system, Amma was called to the front office for a phone call. She left us in our seats but soon came back to gather us, obviously shaken. We waited outside the front entry of the hall for a while, until Cecil Butler and his shiny Lincoln roared up. We hopped in the back and sped off. The power of the car threw us back into the plush leather seats. There were no seatbelts back then, so we bounced around like a couple tennis balls as we screamed into the cool North Carolina night. Cecil dropped Amma off at Cape Fear Valley and took me and Mark home, where a group friends and family had gathered. Our maid, Alumina, who we called Mimi, was there. She was a beloved member of our family.

At age six, I didn't understand social constructs like Jim Crow, but it existed in Fayetteville and was surely the way my grandparents saw the world. But there was no prejudice in my heart, especially for Mimi. She too suffered hard times after Granddaddy passed. Amma could not afford to keep her employed. We would bring her around for occasional work when we could afford it, but that became increasingly rare.

When Amma got home from the hospital, everyone gathered in the dining room. She took me and Mark and drew us close, then made her announcement. I remember Mark bursting into tears, as did some of the women who were present. But what I remember most was Mimi crying and screaming, "That man, that man, that man . . . dear lord Jesus, that man!"

It makes me tear up to this day. I was ashamed to have anyone see me cry, so I jumped off Amma's knee and ran to the back bedroom to cry alone. Mrs. Baker, our next-door neighbor, followed and tried to console me. I was grateful that she did.

I don't remember Mom being there at that moment. Maybe she was out. But she was devastated when she got home. Granddaddy was her hero, too. She had a contemptuous relationship with Amma. Mom was stunningly beautiful and athletic. Men swarmed around her. I think Amma was jealous. But after Granddaddy left us, there was competition between Amma and Mom to be the mother figure to me and Mark. Mom worked all the time, and Amma ran the household, so there was often maneuvering for the top spot. It would only get worse in the coming years.

Mom was the girl that everyone liked. The only child of my grandparents, she was petite and pretty, athletic, had great brunette hair, and always sported a rich tan. Her high school sweetheart was a guy named Bobby whose father owned a local car dealership, so he had money and a cool car. Mom was a majorette at Fayetteville High School, but swimming and water skiing were her preferred activities. She and Bobby were a cute couple. After graduation, Bobby went to University of North Carolina at Chapel Hill, or UNC as we called it, where all rich kids went in North Carolina. Mom decided to give East Carolina a try. She wasn't academically inclined, but that didn't mean she wasn't smart. Although her grades were mediocre, she proved in later years to have considerable analytical capabilities. Self-esteem inhibited her—not smarts. So, off Mom and Bobby went in separate directions. Sadly, this was the end of their love affair.

She wasn't sure what she wanted at East Carolina. As so often happens with one's first taste of real freedom, college social life became the priority, and that's how she met Jay. Like Bobby, Jay came from money; apparently, he was the only rich kid in North Carolina not to end up at UNC. Beautiful women attract wealthy men, and his family basically owned a county somewhere in the state, and he got a Corvette on his sixteenth birthday. Jay was attracted to Mom. Mom was attracted to Jay. One night in 1962, during her freshman year, they proved it.

Granddaddy was furious. Not only was his only daughter pregnant, but now she had to marry this individual, quit school, and do the socially acceptable thing. I know little of this period of our lives. It was something we didn't discuss. It was the past. The last time I saw Jay, my biological father, was in 1969. I was in the second grade, I believe. He gave me a leather jacket and a stack of record albums— Richie Havens, One Man Electrical Band, Janis Joplin, Hendrix. Maybe it was his way of trying to mentor me or say he was sorry.

Shortly after nuptials, I came along in January 1963. Brother Mark followed twenty-two months later. Although the marriage was short, I recall a couple places where we settled. The first was a small duplex apartment in Winston-Salem. Jay had gotten a job at a small radio station and was working as a DJ, a cool job in those days. FM radio was the rage. I remember visiting the studio and being intrigued by all the knobs and lights, all of which I was not allowed to touch. The apartment was simple but clean. I remember watching *Batman* on TV. The music attracted me more than the show itself. There was a nice-sized living room, a perpendicular kitchen, a tiled bathroom, and two small bedrooms. One was of course a nursery, complete with cribs for me and Mark. I hated the confines of a crib.

I have no idea how I remember all this.

The next stop was Charlotte, a much bigger radio market. Jay was moving up in the world. I clearly remember the house, a common ranch style that was popping up all over the state at the time. Brother Mark rented a similar one when stationed in Jacksonville while serving in the Marine Corps in the 1980s. Most importantly, we had a beautiful German shepherd named Duke. We would go for car rides with me and Duke sitting in the back. Jay would open the window for Duke to look out and bark.

One day, Amma and Granddaddy visited. As they left, I recall running to the front storm door crying, not wanting them to go. As I made contact with the door, the glass shattered and opened a long gash on my left wrist. All went into panic mode. I recall everyone being in the bathroom while I sat on Jay's lap as he wiped blood from the wound and picked shards of glass out from the cut. I still have the scar. When people see it, they shy away, probably thinking I attempted suicide. I've never given anything like that a second of thought.

This is where things began to crumble for Mom and Jay.

Before Mom passed in 2018, we talked about this time in her life. She told me that she always felt that Jay had a penchant for other women. He surely had a passion for alcohol. When they got to Charlotte, she thought drugs became part of the menu. All of her assumptions proved true. A few years before this conversation with Mom, I searched and found Jay online. He was living in California. He was in his early seventies at this point. He had remarried, raised a family, and had a successful career in real estate. I cautiously approached him with my first email, making sure that he knew I came in peace.

I wanted nothing more than information. I expressed disappointment that he had abandoned us all those years ago. I learned that he never paid child support. I told him I was determined to never follow his example with my children. He offered to answer any questions I had but offered nothing on his own. We communicated a few times. There was never a sense of relationship between the two of us, just two men sharing email. I felt nothing, no emotional attachment. I thought anger would be part of the equation, but that was never true. I began to get a sense that I had become a bother, or his current family was warning him I may want some sort of restitution.

At the end of my conversation with Mom in 2018, she told me there was emotional and physical abuse in the relationship. At that point, I stopped communication with him. Jay is now what he was then: persona non grata. A man who raises his hand to a woman, his wife, is void of character. It was best to walk away.

I learned at a very young age that relationships always change, and disappointment and sadness are a part of life. When Granddaddy died, although I did not feel abandoned, I lost the security and safety he had provided. We all did. As he declined physically, he could no longer give the attention that he had prior. I remember the loneliness and sadness of watching him struggle. I think I went into another world when he died. I needed to find safety again, to fill that empty feeling in my gut.

Jay's abandonment was different, yet equally hard. I didn't know him. I remember so many small segments of time about him, but I mostly remember his anger. I was learning to deal with disappointment and loss, no-shows at Christmas and birthdays. At that age, you don't understand; you just feel empty. Even sadder to me is that I often wondered if there was something wrong with me. Why didn't he want to be with me? No matter how hard the women in my family tried to make him irrelevant, the emptiness remained, and I think it affected my relationships my entire life. *Am I good enough to be loved?* I would often wonder.

The concept of safety in a relationship is a huge hurdle to clear, and it took decades to find that safety, via my precious wife. Still, I struggle with the issues of his abandonment and push it away as far as I can because even in 2018, he proved he didn't care.

So, I think back to that day of mowing the sand and the arrival of the Corvette. There we all stood, in the summer heat, sizing up one another. Paul Fisher was statuesque and strong. Honorable. Father-like. A man who would not abandon responsibilities. He had to be that guy. He was a paratrooper and a company commander in the 82nd Airborne Division. He had spent a year in Vietnam with another famous unit, the 173rd Airborne Brigade. I recognized the unit and combat patches on his uniform; they were familiar symbols around Fayetteville. As he and Mom sped off that day, I felt there was something between us—at least, I secretly hoped so, and I knew Mark did, too.

CHAPTER 2

A New Family

As we approached Christmas of 1971, we all saw a change in Mom. She was happy and optimistic. After all, the 1960s had been tough on all of us. She was dividing her time between work, time with me and Mark, and Paul. She would do things that never happened in the past, like baking. Well, she attempted to bake. With all of her newfound enthusiasm, we learned that Amma was truly the cook in the family. Trust me, this wasn't something that hurt Mom's feelings. In later years, we joked that when you have Boston Market every Thanksgiving for a decade, the battle for culinary competence is over.

At Christmas, Mom decided that she was going to "make" gifts for me and Mark. I thought, *How in the hell is she going to make Hot Wheels?* The Secret Christmas Gift Shop was being operated at our friend Mark Mathews's house across a field, about a hundred yards from our place. Mark Mathews was a cool guy and a good friend. He was one of those people who was better than you at everything important to a nine-year-old—football, basketball, baseball, board games. We liked him anyway.

His mom, Linda, was a tall brunette who, like my mom, had no problem attracting men. In fact, her claim to fame was that she dated Jeffrey McDonald, the Special Forces doctor who was convicted of killing his family. She wore a lot of makeup and had really big hair that would stand up to anything seen in the 1980s, and boobs the size of cantaloupes. At age nine, I was starting to notice such things, and little did I know that I would learn more about her anatomy than I could ever assume.

Everything at the gift shop was "Top Secret" of the strictest order! Neither of us were allowed at Mark Mathews's place until after Christmas. Torture! But with the confines placed upon us, our imaginations ran wild with the possibilities of what we would find under the tree on the big day. "Maybe Mom is making us a cool racetrack for our Hot Wheels that we could play with in front of the fireplace? Maybe Mom is just using the shop to hide new bikes? Wouldn't it be cool if we got BB guns? Gee, I hope she hasn't learned to knit."

The big day came, and per usual, Mark and I were up at the crack of dawn, dying to see what was under the tree. There were no big or oddly shaped boxes. We began the gift-giving ritual, and it was a little disappointing—socks, underwear, school clothes, and a football. But then it was time. Mom pulled her gift from under the tree. Mark and I approached and began to tear away wrapping paper. Whatever was in there fit in a standard shirt box.

Inside, to our surprise, was a decoupage picture of her. When you have grand illusions of screaming down the road on your new banana-seat, three-speed chopper bike, screaming like banshees while taking out targets with your new Red Ryder BB gun, with at least 100 Hot Wheel cars in your saddlebags, a picture of your mother is a little disappointing.

Maybe Mom knew something. As I write, that picture sits on a library table next to my desk so I can see it as many times a day I wish. In the picture, you see in her eyes and on her face the happiness and enthusiasm, anticipation of the life ahead of us. When cancer took her in 2018, the disease devoured her. In this picture, she is healthy and strong, beautiful and vibrant. It is the way I want to remember her, so this picture will be in my home forever. It is now my favorite Christmas gift ever.

The true gift that Christmas was that Mom and Paul announced their engagement. There was logic to their timing. Paul was coming to the end of his time at Fort Bragg. The Army was going send him to school in the summer of 1972, and then to his next operational assignment. So, at Christmas they announced a February wedding. Two months!

You can imagine the stir this caused, mostly in Amma. It became apparent to her that Mom intended to marry and move with me and Mark in tow. Mom was going to take us away. I remember Amma asking Mom if that was what she intended, and seeing the disappointment and hurt on her face when Mom replied, "They are my sons." This started an emotional battle with all of us. Mark and me had to deal with loyalties to both the mother and grandmother who had been the center of our world. I remember being excited at the prospect of the wedding and having a dad and the possibility of seeing other places, but we also saw and felt Amma's pain.

She and Mom started to fight often; sometimes it was physical. One morning while we got ready for school, Amma and Mom began to argue, we can only assume why. But it escalated, and Amma slapped Mom on the face. Mom countered by punching Amma in the chest while holding a hairbrush. Afterward, they both retreated to safe areas of the house. Mom dressed quickly and left for the day. I vividly remember the fear and confusion it caused. I felt helpless.

Even with the emotions surrounding the wedding, there was a fury of activity around preparation. Amma made Mom's gown and all the bridesmaid dresses. I remember her complaining that her fingers hurt from all the embroidery. Mom and her bridesmaids would come over to the house for almost daily fittings and adjustments. It was hard to concentrate on *Gilligan's Island* on TV with all the hubbub around us.

Before the announcement and during the feverish rush in

January to prepare, we began spending time with Paul, who from then on would be referred to as Dad—a badge well deserved. Dad was and is a good man, and he was determined to not only be a good husband but also be a good father to me and Mark. He accepted the responsibility and, with that commitment, quickly earned our affection. Most men, smug in their lives as bachelors, would never give it all up for a wife and two kids. He even traded in his Corvette for a 1972 Chevrolet Impala so we finally had a car that would accommodate all four of us. This act alone deserved sainthood. He came to baseball games and football games. He coached us on how to throw a curveball and how to throw a proper body block. And he introduced us to golf. We often went to his apartment. Mom would make dinner, and we would have family time around the big console TV. When his roommate Dan McKinney, a great Special Forces officer and winner of the Silver Star, moved out, Mark and I had a room there as well.

Paul was also generous. An Army captain was rich—in our eyes, anyway. I remember him buying Mark a blue baseball glove. Mine was yellow. Yellow! Well, it was the 1970s, so yellow was modern and modern was cool. He bought Mom a set of golf clubs and they began playing together. He also started to take me and Mark out on the links. One day he allowed Mark to skip school and play golf, and another day it was my turn. It was intimate time together. He was showing a real interest in us, and we became closer. It was special and something I will never forget.

We always went to Ryder Golf Course on Fort Bragg. Ryder was the officers club course and the place where I learned the game. On the first tee, about a hundred yards on the right side of the fairway, was a young pine tree maybe six feet high. The fairway took a pretty sharp turn to the right after the tree. Paul would always tell me to aim at the tree when teeing off.

That tree is still there but mature now and at least sixty feet tall. Every time I return to Fort Bragg, I go by the club and look at our tree and send a picture to Dad. Even when we aren't getting along sometimes, the picture helps steady things.

Paul became, and remains, my true father. A father is the man who is there for his children. Biology only plays a small part. I always tell him, "I am the man I have become because of the love, guidance, and opportunity you provided."

Dad came from a different world. He was the second child in a family of eight children, three boys and five girls. A strict Irish Catholic, he actually spent a year in seminary. For the first time in my life, I met people who defined themselves through their European ancestry. Dad's father, Poppie, was from Wales, and his mother, Nanna, was Irish. In the South, we just thought we were all Southern. Even more strange is that they hailed from Upstate New York. Yankees! But their true identity was they were an Army family.

At age twenty-eight, Poppie served in the infantry and military police during World War II and held a commission. Like Dad, he spent time in a famous unit, 11th Airborne Division, where he saw combat in the Pacific. When the war ended, like many who decided to remain on active duty, he had to give up his commission and became a noncommissioned officer—a sergeant. That must have been a hard pill to swallow, but he had a big family to feed. He retired a master sergeant in the Quartermaster Corps in 1963. His final duty station, which became the home for all this clan, was Colonial Heights, Virginia. Transplanted Yankees.

During his career, he shuffled his large family to a number of places, most notably Fort Knox, Kentucky, and Stuttgart, Germany. At Fort Knox, and because of the size of the family, they lived in a refurbished Army barrack, World War II–era wooden structures. In Germany, they lived "on the economy," as we would say, meaning in a German town. While there, Dad learned German.

Dad and Poppie had a difficult relationship, and I think it helped Paul to be a better father for me and Mark, determined not to make the same mistakes. Poppie was tough, emotionally distant, and a bit self-absorbed. I'm not sure if the war played a part in this, but he rarely showed affection or gave praise, something that Dad did well.

Dad told me Poppie would tell the boys to police the yard and have it ready for inspection upon his return in the evening. As he would leave for work, he would throw a cigarette butt somewhere into the yard, and God help you if you didn't find and retrieve the butt. To make matters worse, Poppie would wait until late, like after midnight, to wake the boys and have them go out in the yard with flashlights to redo their poor policing. Barbaric. This was the old Army. But this had a major effect on Dad. I can't imagine the stress and anxiety it caused his brothers and sisters. This is why children leave home and never return.

Years later, Dad often expressed a need to mend things with Poppie. In his old age, Poppie mellowed and was more forthcoming with affection and praise, but it was clear that all his children had anger issues with him.

Sadly, Poppie's wife, Nanna, died in 1989, eight years before he did, and his behavior afterward was a major source of angst. I was in Germany at the time, and only got small portions of the drama from Mom, but Poppie acquired several girlfriends after Nanna died, to the frustration mainly of Dad's sisters. It was the self-absorbed thing. At my first wedding in 1991, however, I remember Dad facing off with Poppie, looking him in the eye, and saying "I love you." The look on Dad's face, even in his fifties, was of a child needing his father's approval. Poppie returned the gesture and they both hugged. But the cuts were very deep, and this was a mere Band-Aid.

Nanna was the strength of their home. She was able to fend off Poppie's childishness and protect the kids. Dad adored her. He loved making her laugh and was devastated when she passed. When she died, I remember getting notification from the Red Cross. I was a young infantry officer stationed in Germany at the time. My friend George Soberon, who was a fellow officer and staff duty officer (SDO), came to my quarters that night and read the notification to me. We were both platoon leaders in 1st Battalion, 36th Infantry, in Friedberg at the time, the Spartans. I thought that was really a nice thing to do, considering George and I had a very competitive relationship—at least, he thought so. I really wasn't interested.

I called Mom and Dad and we all cried. I was shocked when they asked me not to make the transatlantic journey home for the funeral. It was September 1989. At that point, I had not seen my parents since November the previous year, and I assumed they would want me on the first flight available. They asked me to stay in Germany and come home at Christmas, as originally planned. I understood why, but then again, I didn't.

Dad never had a disparaging thing to say about his mother. With eight children and living on a sergeant's salary, she magically kept everyone fed, clothed, and the house in order. She had a lot of help from the older kids, but you could see the toll on her face. Dad always talked about eating a lot of potatoes and how Nanna would water down spaghetti sauce to make it feed everyone. My mom, when becoming a grandmother and after Nanna passed, took the moniker of Nanna in honor of her. We all called Mom that until she passed.

As you can imagine, eight children created a lot of motion. Carol was the oldest. I never thought she was very nice. Dad, the second child, always said Carol hated him and would get him in trouble for the pleasure of it. Dad and some friends stole sacrament wine from their church once. Carol immediately told Poppie, who was very harsh on Dad. That still makes me angry. The third child was Dad's younger brother Tom, who was tall and handsome.

When we met, he was married to a beautiful redhead who I will call Trudy. Tom was determined to never have children, as many growing up in his situation do, and he left the nest as soon as possible. He was very successful selling restaurant equipment in Hampton

Roads, Virginia. When Trudy asked for children, the marriage ended. It was sad, because we all loved Trudy. Tom has since remarried a wonderful woman and enjoys retirement in Florida.

After Carol, Paul, and Tom came four girls: Marianne, Joanie, Kathy, and Suzie. Four daughters in a row. Can you imagine the drama? All married and had families of their own. Marianne married a great man, settled in Birmingham, Alabama, and is now retired in South Carolina. Kathy and her husband were both civil servants who spent several years in Europe and now are retired in Hampton Roads, Virginia. Suzy and Joanie both stayed close to home, married, and raised families. Last came Dan, the youngest. When I met him, he was the star quarterback of his high school team. He had the strongest arm I had ever seen, easily throwing a football sixty yards on the run. He also stayed close to the family, raised one of his own, and has a successful construction business. Dad's relationship with them was distant for many years—too much stress in their young lives. As they aged, they appear to have become closer. They all traveled great distances to be at Mom's funeral. I will always be grateful for that.

Imagine walking into Nanna and Poppie's house after being accustomed to living with only three other people. First, the house was very similar to ours, built at the same time, and about the same size—yes, the same size. At one time, ten people lived there. There were two small bedrooms downstairs. One was Nanna and Poppie's room, and the other was a shoebox-sized room that barely fit two twin beds. Upstairs in this Williamsburg-style house were two larger bedrooms, with a bath. The largest bedroom was set aside for the three boys. Now, when Mark and I were first introduced, only the youngest boy, Dan, was living in the house, still in high school. So he had the entire upstairs to himself. The other room was for the oldest girls. All the other kids had escaped.

As you entered, there was a small living room with tacky 1960s furniture, all on its last legs. Poppie was normally sitting in his corner recliner. Everyone tried to tread quietly around him, as he would bark if anyone interrupted his TV show of the moment. One Christmas, the kids bought him a headset and a radio so he could tune into TV stations while wearing his headset, tuning out the rest of the world. There would be chaos all around him during family functions, and Poppie would be blissfully clueless, sitting there with headphones the size of California navel oranges on his ears.

Perpendicular to the living room was a dining area the size of the bedroom with the two twin beds. In it were ten wooden chairs tightly positioned around an old table. Maneuvering in the dining room required a lot of squeezing by and shuffling, hips forward.

Adjacent to the dining room was a small, galley-style kitchen where Nanna was normally positioned. You never stop missing someone. Nanna was always happy to see you and met you with a big hug and a kiss. Her Irish eyes were always smiling. It makes me cry to write that. She spoke with a strong New York accent, so when she talked to Dad, it was "Pwal," not Paul. The norm was for her and Dad to have some alone time. Dad would talk, and we would hear Nanna laugh. It was magic.

Just after Christmas 1971, we hopped in the new family automobile and headed north on I-95 to the Richmond, Virginia, area, more specifically Colonial Heights. We pulled up to this simple home in a clearly working-class area of town and got out of the car. There were lots of cars parked outside the house. As we entered, the quietness of the neighborhood was overtaken by sound and motion. Laughter, music, food, drink; after all, they were Irish. Poppie remained motionless in his chair.

In this house, all of Dad's family was present—parents, brothers, sisters, husbands, wives' kids—all of which were now our family. It was wild and exciting, scary, and so unfamiliar, but it was also welcoming. Everyone—well, most everyone—was openhearted and friendly. Accepting. It made me feel happy and safe, but it was also a bit much to handle.

After paying your respect to Nanna and Poppie, it was time to run the gambit of everyone there. Dad's oldest sister, Carol, and her husband, an Army sergeant, and some of their kids were there. She was never very friendly and appeared to be very judgmental, but maybe it was just me. Her husband, being a sergeant, didn't like Dad because he was an officer. I never felt they were very nice. They had two boys and a girl. I never met the girl, but I understood she was very pretty and married a handsome guy who made lots of money. Mark and I got along with Carol's boys but lost touch with them over the years. They stayed close to home, while Mark and I roamed the world.

Dad's brother Tom was tall and handsome, always sporting a 1970s porn moustache. He was funny and had tons of Dad jokes. I liked him. At the time he was living in Virginia Beach with wife, Trudy. They were living the good life; both made plenty of cash, opposite of what he grew up with. It was obvious he was running away from poverty, and his short visit back to Colonial Heights was about as much as he could stand.

Trudy was amazing. She was tall, thin, and beautiful, with brilliant, natural red hair, and pale, freckled Irish skin. We all loved her. As I mentioned, she wanted a child and Tom didn't. After a childhood of living with so little and the often barbaric environment they endured, I can't blame Tom for not wanting the responsibility.

Interesting story about Tom. When I was stationed in Germany, just as we were preparing to deploy to the Persian Gulf to participate in the first Gulf War, Tom and his second wife, Myra, came to Europe. Dad gave him my phone number, and one night as I got home around 8 p.m., the phone rang. It was Tom, quite drunk and somewhere in Frankfurt Airport, I assumed at a bar. He wanted me to pick them up and give them a place to crash. The conversation went something like this:

"Hey, Mike, it's your uncle Tom!"

"No shit!" I said. "Where are you?"

"We are in a bar at Frankfurt Airport, come get us. Your Dad said to call you." Tom replied. *Click!* The handset went to a dial tone.

So, there I was, an hour away from the airport, after working a fifteen-hour day, with no idea where they were in an airport the size of JFK, LaGuardia, and Newark combined, in a city the size of Atlanta, and I had to go find them. And this was many years before cell phones, the internet, satellite communication, and GPS navigation on phones. Also, he had called from the landline phone at the bar. I couldn't even star 69 him back then. I went to bed.

A few days later, I heard from Mom and Dad. "You stranded Tom at the airport?'

I couldn't believe it. They were calling me out on the issue, and of course, Tom had called them and let them know what their offspring had done.

"Mom, you can't tell me he came to Europe without hotel reservations," I said.

"I don't know," said Mom.

"Do you realize he hung up the phone without giving me any detail? Plus, I am an hour from the airport. We are deploying. Even if I had the next day off, we are on a wartime footing. We are going to war. I can't entertain them now."

"Okay," Mom replied.

The conversation with Mom ended, but the angst between Tom and I didn't end until I saw him at Mom's funeral, almost thirty years later. We never crossed paths until that moment. But we did mend fences. I'm glad. He and his wife are really cool people.

Tom and Myra have lived in some great places, normally close to the ocean. Florida and California are their favorites. Financially independent, they have transitioned to retired life, doing small community jobs in their spare time. One cool job they had was running the trailer park in Southern California where Matthew McConaughey once lived. Tom and Myra would use large water hoses to help fight off paparazzi, helping give Matthew a little privacy. It was when he was filming the movie *Surfer, Dude*. Alright, alright, alright!

As for the four girls younger than Dad and Tom:

Marianne is wonderful and she married a great guy named Al. He spent a year in Vietnam as well. I have many fond memories of them. At this time, they had a baby boy named Thad, who was cute and so smart. You could tell that he was observant and able to soak in much of the adult environment around him. As an adult, he became a great chef in Houston. I love it when people follow passion and creativity, and not money and power.

Often, Marianne would put Thad in her Volkswagen bug and visit us if we were somewhere near Birmingham, Alabama, where they lived for many years. She visited at Fort Gordon, Georgia, prior to us leaving for Thailand, and Biloxi, Mississippi, after we returned. She was always fun. Marianne and Al also have twins, a boy and a girl, that sadly I have never met. They appear to be great people on Facebook. Army families, because of constant relocation, have these issues.

In truth, Cathy, Joanie, and Susie are a blur to me. But they are all good people, married with families. All stayed in Virginia, and they did their best. Cathy and her husband, both government servants, went to Germany for a few years. All I can say is that they were all very nice to Mark and me, especially at this initial meeting.

Baby Dan, Dad's youngest brother, was the quarterback at Colonial Heights High School at the time. He had a nice girlfriend whom he married, named Cathy. They eventually had two children, neither of whom I have met. Of all the Fisher kids, he was the one with the most opportunity. He was "the man" in high school and a quarterback at a very large school. But he chose to stay home.

He was exciting to be around. And he had an arm like a rocket.

In these later years, his health has started to decline. He chose to be a contractor, and the daily physical grind took its toll. I wonder if there are any regrets.

Of all eight siblings, Dad is the only one who was formally educated. After graduating from high school, he attended seminary for a year but left to sow wild oats. He went to community college for two years and then to East Tennessee State University to finish a bachelor's degree. At ETSU, Dad paid his way. He worked and joined a fraternity, Sigma Phi Epsilon. The fraternity allowed him to live for free if he acted as the house manager, running the kitchen, managing the house budget, lawn work, and cleaning the house—with the help of pledges, of course. He earned his commission as a signal officer through ROTC there, and left for a career as an Army officer.

As I said earlier, Dad spent a year in Vietnam, first with the 299th Combat Engineers, famous for fighting off a major North Vietnamese attack that included Soviet-made PT-76 tanks. Then he spent time with the famous 173rd Airborne Brigade, Sky Soldiers, who have been in the news a lot over the past two decades for having four Medal of Honor winners who fought in Iraq and Afghanistan. That's far more than any other unit. Dad became a telecommunications engineer later in his career and held the highest security clearance. I am proud of my dad. Being a Sky Soldier defined him. Dad was and remains a paratrooper.

This was an exciting and new time for me. I am sure Mark felt the same. So many changes, so many different perspectives, a new family, the possibility of leaving Fayetteville and Amma, a new and very different family just a few hours away.

I don't remember fear, though. This, in all its complexity, was the right opportunity, a chance to see other shores, and I was ready.

CHAPTER 3

Hard Goodbyes

Wedding day came quickly. Mark and I got up early with Amma, had breakfast, and then put on our best "Sunday, go-to-meeting" clothes. Mark wore a nice navy, three-piece suit and penny loafers. I, on the other hand, looked like a vinyl siding salesman. I wore a green hound's-tooth blazer, olive-drab-green trousers, a yellow dress shirt the color of my baseball glove, and a horrible green-and-yellow striped tie. To top that off, I wore brown, wing-tip shoes and had a haircut that would make Moe from the Three Stooges jealous. I looked and felt ridiculous.

Before the ceremony, I slipped into the room where the bridesmaids were changing and saw something that truly startled me. This wasn't planned. I remember all the air leaving my body, like I'd stuck a fork in a light socket. I couldn't move. As I walked in, there in all her magnificent glory, naked as a jaybird, was Linda Mathews and her boobs, and the world's largest 1970s porn bush. I was enthralled and terrified at the same time.

At first, no one saw me. All of Mom's other bridesmaids were chatting and laughing. I ignored them, and they didn't see me. What I was seeing had a physical and emotional effect that I had never felt. I slipped to the corner of the room and continued to stare. Things, the right things, jiggled. They seemed to sway as she moved. It was like I was looking at the Southern version of Linda Richmond, Mike Myer's *Saturday Night Live* character—Jewish, big hair, lots of makeup, always self-grooming. But I wasn't interested in her giant, football helmet hairdo.

Then, a great gasp. *Shit, I've been found out!* One of the bridesmaids saw me. Mom grabbed me by the collar and escorted me out. I didn't see her coming. I only felt a strong jerk on my arm, which resulted in me being flung out the door.

"Boy, don't make me spank your ass in front of God and everybody!" Mom barked.

"Mom, I just wanted to see you!"

Damn. Didn't she know how such things are important life lessons for nine-year-old boys? I didn't know these things were significant until I saw them, but in one moment, I had learned how girls, and their parts, made me feel. I had just been introduced to one thing that would rule my entire life. It would influence most of my bad decisions from that day forward. Why else would I remember the moment so clearly?

The ceremony was at the Main Post Chapel on Fort Bragg. The chapel, built during the war, was placed in Normandy Village, the area where all senior commanders lived, from the commander of 18th Airborne Corps to all subordinate division, brigade, and battalion commanders. Houses were beautifully built in a Spanish style, with red roofs and yellow stucco outer walls. Lawns were manicured, and everyone had their names on signposts outside their quarters—COL Johnson, LTC and Mrs. Mayweather, the Smith Family. The trees were huge and beautiful, different from our neighborhood. They covered homes like large umbrellas. I immediately knew I wanted to live there one day.

Over the years, the Main Post Chapel would become an icon in my life. I would say goodbye to many friends there, most at a young age and before their time. I still visit every time I find myself at Fort Bragg. The last time I was there in a formal capacity, in the late

1990s, was to say goodbye to a member of a unit I once commanded. The soldier had lost control of his Ford Mustang and rolled it into a ditch. Sadly, the impact broke his neck. One day you are celebrating the beginning of life's journey, the next you are grieving the end.

This day in February of 1972, we were celebrating.

All of Dad's friends were wearing their dress blues, the Army formal uniform, complete with ribbons and badges. The Airborne chaplain who officiated the ceremony wore his blues under his robe. Only Dad's best man, his brother Tom, was in civilian attire—a tux with a puffy shirt. Mom looked beautiful in a yellow gown. There was that color again. I can't remember what color her bridesmaids wore. All I could see was pink, thanks to Linda Mathews.

After the ceremony, photos were taken of the bride and groom, the bride and bridesmaids, the groom and groomsman, the bride and groomsman, etc. *Aren't we supposed to go have cake?* Then it was our turn.

Amma, Mark, and I took part in a series of family photos. When seeing the pictures, for the first time in my life I realized I had horrible teeth. Neither Mark nor I had ever been to a dentist. It just wasn't a thing then, or maybe we didn't have the money. I don't know, but I learned that I looked like a vinyl siding salesman with a Three Stooges haircut and hillbilly teeth. How embarrassing. I knew I'd never have a chance with Linda Mathews.

Once we joined the Army family, Mom made sure the dentist became priority. At our first duty station after leaving Fort Bragg, we went to the dentist often. In those days, though, the military dentistry was a little behind the rest of the world. I remember visits being quite uncomfortable. Okay, painful! To make matters worse, the average military dentist didn't care if you were uncomfortable. It was your fault your teeth were fucked up; now stand by for punishment.

Many years later, while I was on active duty and stationed at Fort Riley, Kansas, I had a dentist who refused to talk to me, or anyone. He was a colonel, so he had the authority to be an asshole, but as you entered his office, he would motion you to his chair of torture. Once the procedure was complete, he would motion you out of the chair, hand you a scrip for pain meds or antibiotics, and then turn his back without a word. I felt lucky for the pain meds.

Maybe I am being a little harsh. Dental readiness in the Army was serious business. How can a soldier fight with an abscessed tooth? It would make it difficult to focus on your job. Truth is, I've had dental pain that Jack Daniels couldn't numb, and the Army will not deploy a soldier who is not "dental ready." This means the Army Dental Corps had a huge mission to make every soldier's mouth capable of going overseas and taking care of bad guys. So, part of their schtick was to be a little bossy. They wanted to make visits unpleasant so hopefully people would take care of themselves. Sometimes it worked, sometimes not.

After retiring and going to civilian dentists, I couldn't believe how nice they were. But it was about money then, and I had a choice of who I wanted to see.

Our first experiences with dentists were unpleasant. One day in a dentist chair at Fort Gordon, Georgia, things got a little crazy. The clinic was in an old, World War II–style barracks. The building, constructed of wood, had paint chipping off the walls, and no air-conditioning. To help remedy this issue, they opened every window and door and placed large fans at the ends of each open bay. My chair was next to cargo doors that were on the side of the barrack. You were basically being tortured for everyone to see. As the dentist dug in my mouth, enjoying watching me squirm, someone ran past the open cargo door at full sprint. Everyone stopped and looked.

Then we heard "Halt, or I will shoot!" and two MPs ran past the doors with their service pistols drawn, M1911, .45 caliber, the kind that makes big holes in people, not the 9mm crap they use today.

Again, my dentist didn't budge. So, there I sat, in pain and terrified that I would witness a wayward hippie getting shot by two Vietnam-era draftees who would have probably enjoyed it. It was a little stressful, but my teeth looked great. The MPs ultimately caught the guy and arrested him, no shots fired. Let the torture continue.

After the wedding, the next stop was the reception, which took place at the beautiful, Spanish-style officers club on Fort Bragg. There was a band and a large buffet, and of course cake. Everyone was in party mode. I remember many soldiers dressed in their finery, accompanied by their wives or dates. Dad invited all his sergeants and officers to the party. He was still a commander in the 82nd at the time. The party would surely get a little wild.

When we got there, Mark, Amma, and I immediately turned and left. I am not sure why. Was it Mom and Dad saying there would be alcohol and maybe the kids shouldn't be a part of things? Or was it Amma feeling uncomfortable, needing to take us to a place that was safe in her eyes? I don't know, but there was no cake for us that day. I was really disappointed. I felt left out. I needed to be with Mom and Dad, but the adults in the equation were maneuvering for position, and we were the pawns. Now I couldn't have cake or Linda Mathews.

The days and weeks after the wedding went by fast. During this period, me and Mark spent time with both Amma and Mom, who was living full-time with Dad. We went on a vacation to Sunset Beach a few weeks before leaving North Carolina. It was a happy trip, but it was the first time I experienced Dad's anger and discipline. Adjacent to where we were staying was an arcade. In the evenings, Mom and Dad would allow us to go there and hang out, shoot pool, and play pinball. One day, Dad only had three quarters to give us for the arcade. He gave us instructions to share them equally. Being the older brother, I kept two and gave Mark only one, which pissed him off. He immediately ran to Dad and said I didn't share the quarters, which was not true. How do you divide a quarter?

What happened then scared me, though. Dad grabbed me by

the shoulder, forcefully spun me around, and to Mark's delight smacked me on my ass several times. He then forcefully sat me down in the corner and angrily told me to stay until released. I felt like the family dog. Very military. Probably how his father acted. The spanking didn't hurt, but the manner did. For the first time, I saw how he reacted to negative stimulus. Dad had an explosive temper, and when he was angry, he was physical. I sat in the corner of the room, tears in my eyes. His wrath increased in time, usually fueled by his love of Johnny Walker Red.

From an early age, alcohol was a part of our lives. Dad's family were Welsh-Irish, and alcohol consumption was a daily event. In college, it was the backbone of the social environment. And in Vietnam, it was the way you relieved stress. So, these habits were not only ingrained—they were the norm. Alcohol and a steady hand when dealing with children rarely mix. It causes variation in behavior of the parent and uncertainty and fear in the child. We never knew at what level Dad would react. We walked on eggshells around Dad at times, trying to find a comfortable and safe place.

Dad wasn't the only one to administer corporal punishment. Amma surely lit us up when we deserved it—with switches and the occasional belt. Mom would smack us on the ass with her hand, and Mom was strong. But it was the anger and the fury that scared me and guided my behavior and my relationship with Dad for many years.

Spankings came if we were late for dinner, if we made a mess, if we made too much noise. Normally it was a belt, but one day, he couldn't find his belt, so he went into a closet and got a wire hanger, which he elongated. It caused welts on our legs and backside. When Mom saw the welts, she went into action, telling Dad that if his behavior didn't change, this experiment was over and she would take me and Mark back to Fayetteville, and she would go, too. I always respected Mom for that. I don't know what fueled his anger. I have always assumed it was the combination of life with his father and combat in Vietnam. I never wanted to believe that it also had to do with being self-absorbed and liking scotch just a little too much. I think all these things were a part of the equation.

Dad really tried to get better, and I truly respect him for that. He accepted the responsibility of taking on a wife and her two kids. The pressure on him must have been incredible. One moment, he was single, with a Corvette and plenty of money; the next, he was trying to adjust to being broke on the tenth day of the month. But most importantly, when Mom faced off with him, he didn't do what nearly all childish men would do—walk away. He listened and tried to improve.

I am so glad. I couldn't imagine life without him. And I don't mean to demonize him. I made a million mistakes with my kids, ones that I regret and pray over and cry about to this day. I love all six of them and would give my life for them on any day. I know that's a bit dramatic, but it's true. What's truly important in the life of a parent? The children. Dad hung in there. He listened. He learned, but most importantly, he loved. Praise God.

Mom's other demon was Amma, and their battles lingered. A few months after we moved, Amma came to Augusta for Christmas. During dinner one night, Amma and Dad got into an argument over Mark's and my hair length, of all things. Dad ended up walking away from the dinner table. Amma decided to take offense. It started a ridiculous Hatfield and McCoy–style feud that lasted to the day she died.

The day came. For the first time in my life, I was leaving Fayetteville. I remember always dreaming of travel. I thought the map of North Carolina was just a backwards US map, with our Outer Banks reversed, lining up with the West Coast, the northern border with Virginia like the northern border with Canada, and the Piedmont looking similar to how Texas borders Mexico. We had a Florida, but it stuck out straight, not downward. I always knew I wanted to see the world and yearned for the day I would leave North Carolina.

Everything we had fit in a couple of suitcases. What furniture Dad had was moved by the Army, but when we left Amma's house, all we owned fit in the trunk of a 1971 Chevrolet Impala. We didn't take any toys. We didn't really have any, except our baseball gloves. The day our life changed took maybe ten minutes of preparation. Dad came over early. Mom had stayed the night with us at Amma's. The house had a heavy, sad feeling, kind of like when Granddaddy died. We loaded the car and met in the living room to say goodbye. Amma cried uncontrollably. I did, too. All I know is that she had to get out of the house. She had jury duty. She quickly went to her car and sped out of the driveway, still weeping. Mark and I just stood there and watched her drive off.

In my life, I have dealt with divorce, combat with a hostile enemy, and chronic disease, but nothing has scared me like the prospect of losing a child. And this in many ways was how Amma must have felt. Both Mom and Amma did things to manipulate their relationships with me and Mark in order to be viewed as the preferred parent. I have seen the same behavior in divorce many times. When the stakes are that high, people will do terrible things, even to the most beloved and trusted people in their lives, to win. That day, Amma lost. And no matter who was legally right, her worse fear came true. I know because I have felt that fear and that panic; her life was crushed that day.

There was nothing I could do. I am so sorry, Amma. I am so sorry.

Mom and Dad tried their best to make us feel better, but the drive to Georgia was long. They told us stories and jokes, anything to keep our minds off what had just happened. We were on our way to Augusta, Georgia, home of the Masters golf tournament. Actually, Dad was going to school at Fort Gordon. Officers and NCOs in the

Army have academic requirements and qualifying jobs at each step of their careers for advancement to a new grade or rank. Dad had just finished his branch-qualifying job as a company commander at Fort Bragg. Now he was going to the appropriate academic course, the Signal Officers Advanced Course. As a lieutenant, his branch-qualifying job was serving as a platoon leader, an organization of about thirty people.

Life in Georgia, from a visual perspective, wasn't much different from Fayetteville. We were still in the South. We moved into a townhouse apartment with three bedrooms and a bath. There were military families all around with many kids. The only differences were that Amma was far away, and we lived with Mom and Dad full-time. This took adjustment.

Both Mark and I went to Roy E. Rollins Elementary School in Augusta. Unlike North Carolina schools, Georgia schools had not yet desegregated. In my third-grade class, there not a single Black child, but we had a Black teacher, a beautiful and kind woman named Ms. Stokes. To show you how children are taught prejudice, which is not innate, every one of the White children in that class adored her. There was never any drama associated with the color of her skin. I loved her, too. When I first got to the class, I was still very emotional about leaving Amma. I would sit in class and cry. I could not help it, nor could I stop. Ms. Stokes would kindly explain to the children why I was upset, and because they respected her, no one was cruel to me. She made everything alright.

Every morning, Ms. Stokes would send one student to the bookstore so kids could purchase needed supplies. Most of the time, children just wanted to buy the cherry cough drops so they could sit in class and eat candy. It was the drug that pacified the masses. Cough drops were a dime, but I never had money and had to survive each day watching everyone happily suckle their sweet cherry treat. Ms. Stokes, noticing this, one day bought me a box. It made me feel welcome. I will always be grateful. From that point, and because of that kind gesture, I began to cope with my new life and became a functioning member of the class.

It was hard adjusting to life at home as well, but Mom and Dad worked hard to help. They did a great job making the apartment comfortable. In the living room, there was a nice couch and two high-back chairs. Focal point of the room was a huge console TV, the type that you needed a forklift to move. Dad had a stereo, so we often had music in the house. He had a keen ear for music and was a great dancer. This is where I started to love soul music: the Temptations, Sly and the Family Stone, Otis Redding, the O'Jays—the list went on and on. The house was always full of music. Family dinners were the norm. Mark and I played baseball and were in Cub Scouts. Mark, Dad, and I would build model airplanes and watch TV together. There was a community pool where families gathered. It was very social.

On Saturday morning, me and Mark would get up early, fix ourselves bowls of cereal and watch cartoons quietly so as to not wake up Mom and Dad. Life was pretty good, but we always missed Amma.

Mom and Dad loved having dinner parties, and many of the folks who frequented our house were officers from other countries, in the States to attend Army schools. We met officers from Jordan, the Philippines, and one special one from Thailand. His name was Aswan, and he was a Royal Thai Army paratrooper, so of course Dad was attracted to him immediately. He was an impeccable officer. The Thai military is one to be taken seriously. If it were not for the strength of their beloved King Rama the Ninth, and the quality of their military, their country, like all others in Southeast Asia during the twentieth century, would have suffered greatly.

Aswan came from a prominent family. He was superbly educated, and his father was a general officer in the Royal Thai Army. So, he was well connected. Little did we know that he would play a very important role in our safety in the coming years. All the foreign officers we met were the finest officers their countries had to offer, and so Mark and I began an education beyond the scope of poor kids from North Carolina.

Assignments time came at the end of Dad's schooling. Since he had completed two assignments with combat units, it was time for him to do something different. At this moment in history, most of the Army was forward deployed, either fighting the war in Vietnam or standing toe-to-toe with the Soviets in Europe. We assumed that going overseas was possible, and we talked about going to Europe, which would have been amazing. There was always the prospect of Dad going to Korea for a year, but that would have left Mom, Mark, and I alone in Georgia. Tours in Korea were one year in length, and unaccompanied, meaning Dad couldn't bring us with him.

Out of the blue, Dad's assignments officer offered him Thailand, in Southeast Asia, next door to all the ruckus in Vietnam. Mark and I, other than meeting Aswan, had no idea what or where the hell Thailand was. But after some family discussion and a little research, we all said yes to traveling halfway around the world and living there for the next three or four years. We might as well have been going to Mars.

And just like that, the school year was over. Dad graduated from his school, the movers came and got our stuff, and we were off. Of course, the first thing was to say goodbye to Amma. I have often wondered if Mom and Dad chose Asia, at least in part, to distance themselves from the drama surrounding Amma. Amma could be in Germany in eight hours, Washington DC in five, and Fort Hood, Texas, in eight. Bangkok was twenty-four hours away. We got about as far away from Fayetteville as possible.

The goodbye was hard, but I don't remember it being overly emotional. At that point, after living in Georgia for six months, we had developed a veneer when confronted with the situation. The goodbye was merely a formality, but it was serious. We were going halfway around the world. Unless Amma decided to make the journey, and she never did, even when Mom and Dad offered to foot the bill, we would not see her for a long time. It turned out to be three and a half years.

Before leaving the US, we spent a couple of days hanging out in San Francisco. I remember it being cold and rainy. We ate at the Fisherman's Wharf. I loved the sourdough bread. We took pictures of us on some old ship. Both Mark and I had shoulder-length hair— very '70s.

In those days, airplanes didn't have the range that they do today. Modern aircraft can fly for twenty hours if needed. The flight schedule for us then was San Francisco to Honolulu, Honolulu to Guam, Guam to Manila, Manila to Saigon, and finally, Saigon to Bangkok. If you needed sleep, you had a comfortable economy class seat to enjoy. So, time to suck it up.

I remember the hop from Honolulu to Guam seeming like it took a month, and we did not see land the entire time. As we got closer to land, the hops got shorter. The flight from Manila to Saigon was less than two hours. Heaven!

Landing in Saigon those days was a bit precarious. As a kid, living next to Fort Bragg and watching Walter Cronkite on TV and listening to Dad and his friends, I picked up on military terminology like a magnet. In fact, I was close to being a pro. I knew what an "arch light strike" was: a B-52 bomber raid; an "ambush"; an airborne assault; and that "humping the pig" meant carrying the M-60 machine gun. It was a part of my life. I also knew that a "Hot LZ" (landing zone) meant that where we were landing was being attacked. More importantly, I knew if they were shooting at an airport, airplanes were the biggest prize. And obviously, we were landing inside the biggest prize.

As we entered South Vietnamese airspace, I recall the flight crew announcing calmly, "Okay, everyone, the LZ in Saigon is HOT, so when we land, we will taxi as fast as possible and leave the engines running. As soon as we stop and have stairs for you to depart, we need you to get off the plane, as fast as possible."

What? I was ten years old, and we were landing in a hot LZ! We hadn't even gotten to Bangkok, and I was already rethinking things.

When we landed, I remember people running off the airplane, people running on the airplane, and an immediate departure. It happened fast. The air crew was stern and efficient. Focused. At first, I was scared and panicked a little. But I watched Dad, and he handled it well. It took me a few minutes, but I calmed. I decided to handle it. Mark didn't know what was happening.

What a day! My first in a combat zone.

I have a theory that the more stress you are exposed to, if you can handle it, the stronger you become. Although this event was unforeseen, I think I am stronger for it. You get scared, then you gain composure and deal with the issue. I have been in many such predicaments.

Today, I joke with Dad about the incident, saying that I too am a Vietnam veteran.

Bangkok was a short hour and half away. Flying out of South Vietnamese airspace was a relief. We were exhausted, and all we wanted to do was find a bed. As we landed at Don Muang airport outside of Bangkok, we all just stared ahead like zombies. Hot, humid air hit my face as the aircraft door opened. We grabbed our things and shuffled off the plane. Little did we know that compared to Bangkok, the incident in Saigon would prove to be more like a day at Disney. When we entered the crowded terminal, Mark and I were no longer just poor kids from the South. Our real education had begun.

CHAPTER 4

Superhighway

The midday heat was stifling. As we walked outside the airport terminal, our bodies exploded in perspiration. Our first moments in Thailand were a flood of sights, sounds, and smells. Thousands of people were hustling through their day. It was a sea of humanity, vendors on the street, and students on their way home from school—major traffic. It was exciting, overwhelming, and beautiful. The air was full of the sounds of people talking in a foreign language, the smells of street food, and vehicle exhaust. We soon learned that days in the high nineties and even higher humidity were the norm.

Our new world was vibrant, colorful, and loud. Thankfully, we were met by our sponsor, a kind man named Major Randy Richardson, a senior officer at Dad's new unit. It was a common practice for units to help newcomers adjust and get them settled. We couldn't have been happier to see him. I, for one, would have no idea what to do or where to go if left to my own devices.

Major Richardson had thankfully enlisted the use of an OD-green Army passenger van for our first venture into the city. The interior was basic, sparse, and clean with plastic seats. But, most importantly, the air conditioner worked. We loaded our bags in the rear, piled into the van, and then crept into traffic. In the coming years, we would become very close to the Richardson family. Mark and I became close friends with his sons, Randy and Darrel, and Mom and Dad were close with the major and Mrs. Richardson. They had a fantastic house and would often cook for us. Trust me, this man knew his way around a barbeque pit.

The road that led us from Don Muang airport into the city those days was called a superhighway. Bangkok has grown so much in the past four decades that I doubt the road is still there. It wasn't super at all, just four lanes, two each way, straight, flat, filthy, and no rules. There were no speed limits, no warning signs, and no cops.

The traffic was frantic and extremely dangerous. White public buses, which also served as school buses, packed to the brim with students in their school uniforms were common. Boys were clad in white button-up shirts and royal-blue trousers, with skirts for the girls. I am sure people died traveling like this. There was never any airspace between bodies, and on occasion, folks would hop a ride on the roof, or on the rear cargo ladder of these vehicles. Then there were huge construction and cargo trucks driven by bands of filthy men dressed in rags, eager to get the job done and then get behind a few cold beers and maybe next to a warm body. They were the Thai equivalent of construction workers in New York who spend half their days gawking at women. Gawking would become a common theme.

These men also liked to hassle foreigners, or *falong* in Thai. I remember many times when these assholes would pull their trucks alongside our open window taxi and gun the accelerator to fill the cabin with diesel exhaust. And like the workers in New York, they would smirk at us with devilish grins. Normal traffic included whatever Toyota, Isuzu, or Japanese vehicle was popular, racing down the road at the fastest speed possible, windows open, the driver cussing at anyone in the way. As I learned early on, cursing in Thai is a critical skill for a young falong boy.

And then there were the vehicles that should not be on any road, especially on the superhighway. Mopeds, motorized bikes with small engines that start by using pedals, were widespread. I often wondered how bikes with such small engines kept up with the frantic pace, but they did. I don't know if owners tinkered with engines for extra horsepower or if they could eventually get up to speed when revving engines at full bore, but any mistake on a moped was sure death.

Superhighway was poorly maintained. Potholes were common. Garbage was common. Farm animals were common. Helmets and safety gear were not. One morning, I saw a school student on a moped, following a packed school bus a mere five feet or so from the back bumper. The driver was speeding along with a confident smirk. He kept his craft at full bore as fellow students cheered him on from the back of the bus. I hoped this kid had great reflexes, because I'd bet you a case of beer the brake lights on the bus didn't work. And then there was the most dangerous of all, samlors, often called "tuk tuks" in other parts of Asia. samlors three-wheelers were basically mopeds with a bench seat in back, designed to hold as many riders as possible. Even today, the streets of Bangkok are full of them.

Drivers controlled the craft with a bicycle-like handlebar, and in the rear, there were no side doors and, of course, nothing like a seat belt. Often you would see an entire family in the back of one of those things, screaming down the superhighway. One day a driver, at speed, attempted a sharp turn, and a samlor just rolled and rolled and rolled.

As you approached the city, a weird haze covered the Bangkok skyline. Today, Bangkok has huge skyscrapers. In 1973, the tallest building in town was twenty-two stories, a place called the Chokchai Building. For the times, it was a marvel of engineering, but everyone who inhabited the building prayed that they wouldn't be there during a big earthquake. I know this because Dad's office was in the Chokchai Building the first year of our stay. Can you say, "Not to code?"

The city haze was a mixture of air pollution, dust and dirt, and heat. It covered the city like the dome of Atlantis. As we entered the city, the pace of traffic slowed to a crawl. There were no traffic lights, only the occasional traffic cop in the middle of the clutter, adorned in proper uniform and white gloves, Ray-Ban shooters, and a whistle permanently affixed to the mouth. The cop would frantically try to control matters. Traffic was equally determined to ignore him.

Most Thai buildings of the era were two to three-story row-style dwellings made from cinder block and wood. The bottom floors were open to the streets, and this was where families socialized or ran their businesses. Some of the best meals of my life were made by street vendors there. They futilely attempted to cool these places with fans.

In the evenings, businesses would put tables and chairs on sidewalks to accommodate evening customers. To secure the house at night, owners would pull down security screens, bars, or metal gates and then retire to family living areas on upper floors where air-conditioning was possible. It made for a long, hot day.

It was apparent that most Thais led simple lives, and most would be considered poor in Western terms. But from a Thai perspective, they were just average folks, good Thai people. There was an almost nonexistent middle class, and a very small but very wealthy upper or ruling class. The average Thai, compared to us overfed Westerners, had very little, but it didn't seem to bother them.

When I was there, government buildings were the most lavish, along with Buddhist temples, and hotels. Now Bangkok's skyline rivals the biggest cities in the world.

The Chao Prya Hotel, named for one of the major rivers running through the city, was nine stories, built in the early 1960s. It served as the officers club for all military in the area. It also provided temporary housing for arriving families or those preparing to leave the country. Basically, you arrived in-country, spent a month or so living in the hotel, rested and got acclimated, started school or went to work, found a place to live, then you left the hotel, and your life in Bangkok was underway.

We got to our hotel room for a much-needed rest. In it was two single beds, one for Mark, one for me, our own bath, and a huge picture window overlooking Bangkok. A door connected us with Mom and Dad's room, and a console radio was between the two beds, but no TV. Curious about the radio, I gave it the on-off knob a turn. To all our surprise, "I Left My Heart in San Francisco" was playing, an appropriate tune to lull us all into a deep sleep.

The hotel was really cool. As you walked through electronic sliding front doors, air-conditioned coolness engulfed you. A concierge was to the left, and the room opened into a two-story lobby. Sitting areas with beautiful teak furniture and Thai silk pillows were on the left and right, but your eyes were captured by the long front desk, where eager hotel employees waited to greet you. To the right side of the lobby was the entrance to the bar that often had live entertainment, and sometimes "living entertainment," if you know what I mean. The place was the hub of nighttime activity, downstairs and upstairs.

When you looked up, there was a mezzanine. It became the center of our indoor life. There was a large sitting area where kids staying at the hotel would gather and be "cool." We got off the elevator at the mezzanine because riding the elevator was cool and walking stairs was not. To the right was a jewelry store that sold only stuff made in-country. Mom and Dad bought us all custom-made initialed pinky rings there as a welcoming gift. I lost mine almost immediately because ten-year-old boys don't wear gold pinky rings. But this extravagance was an indication that far more than just our living location was going to change.

The cost of living in Thailand was extremely cheap. Dad at that time, being a senior captain, earned a salary that allowed us to live a life we never dreamed of, hence gold jewelry. But that was only the beginning. On the mezzanine, the Army and Air Force Exchange Service (the PX) had a bookshop and a movie theater. Yes, movies! We could go see a movie every night, for a mere fifty cents. James Bond films were my favorite. Sean Connery, not Roger Moore. Heaven.

Our culinary life was greatly improved as well. On the first floor, just past the front desk, was the hotel's dining room where we would have our fantastic nightly meals, served to us by waiters in white dinner jackets. It was amazing. This was not the Olive Garden. For the first time I tried baked Alaska, a dessert with Neapolitan ice cream, covered in merengue. Get this, when they bought it to your table, they doused it in cognac and lit it flambé. A huge blue flame would brown the merengue, which looked like a big snow-covered mountain in Alaska. It was the most decadent thing I had ever seen.

Outside the hotel was an Olympic-sized swimming pool, with three diving boards. There was also an outdoor bar with chairs, tables, and umbrellas surrounding the pool. Waiters brought you whatever you asked for. Palm trees grew on the outskirts of the compound, but many were planted in large ceramic pots around the seating area, for ambiance. It was made private with high cinder block walls, painted white. The best part was the pool never closed, even during the cool rainy season when the temperature would drop into the fifties in the mountainous northern region of the country. It was common to hear of people freezing to death.

Adjacent to the pool was a snack bar that resembled a diner in the US. It had a long serving counter with stools and booths that lined a wall of plateglass windows. You could order American or Thai fare. The ladies that worked there were awesome. Every day when we got home from school, we would go to the snack bar and they would make us Thai fried rice, or "cowpot." This was the beginning of my love affair with Thai food. To this day, and no matter where I go, I seek out good Thai food, speak what Thai I remember, and enjoy the dishes of my youth.

Mark and I met many people our age in the hotel and made lots of new friends. We would pal around in flocks and enjoy the trappings of our island oasis. In fact, my first kiss was at the Chao Prya. A group of us between the ages of ten and thirteen got together, and suddenly a raging game of spin the bottle began. I sat nervously in the circle, praying that the bottle would never point at me. I was one of the youngest in the game and still very scared of girls.

Then it happened. The bottle pointed at me, and a girl from across the circle started to lunge towards me, lips first. I did what any red-blooded American boy my age would do: I got up and ran like hell. My bros gave me major shit for it, and after ten minutes or so, I gathered all the courage I could muster and rejoined the circle. The bottle continued to spin.

Again, the bottle pointed at me, and a cute and somewhat older girl named Jackie, determined to not let me escape again, grabbed me by the shirt and dragged me towards her room. All I could see was Jackie looking me in the eye, telling me to keep moving. My bros were howling in the background. I was shaking in my boots, I can tell you. I never assumed this was the way it was supposed to happen.

Unlike me, Jackie had already begun to develop into an adult. She was petite and cute, and had all the parts that Linda Mathews had, just different. But her most endearing characteristic was that she was truly a proud young Black woman. Everyone in our group respected her for it, perhaps a little intimidated by her. When she wanted to say something, or have something, she made it clear. She usually got her way. That day, she made it clear that she wanted to spend a little private time with me. Eventually, she got her way.

She walked in the door of her room first. I followed and turned to close it when, as I began to face her, all I saw and felt were her warm lips and body pressed against mine. To add to the ambush, she had a bear hold on me that Hulk Hogan couldn't break. At first, I tried to free myself, but then something profound happened. I realized how awesome this was. I went, "Mmmmmmm," wrapped my arms around her, and snuggled in for the ride. Lots of lessons were learned that day. First, if a girl wants to show you affection, shut up, snuggle in, and enjoy it.

This was an invaluable lesson. Until Dad came along, there were no men in my life. Women ruled the day, and in truth, I was fine with that. Women make things nice and warm. Men make things hard and cold. I chose women. That day, I also learned it doesn't matter who you are, the color of your skin, or what culture; if it involved a woman, it all felt, tasted, and smelled good.

But maybe there was more than the lesson about women.

Maybe I was learning that when you lived in an environment where everyone was basically equal, had all they needed, and you were not subjected to the stifling social norms you were accustomed to, you could move beyond such bias. You could live together without strife. In fact, you could learn to love together.

Little did I realize it, but I was growing up. My life was so small in North Carolina. I was still just a little kid. Before Dad, I had no father, and we were very poor. The new friends, the affluence, the blending of the cultures, plus all the hubbub in Thailand opened a new world I would have never seen had I remained in North Carolina. I felt happy and excited. I was learning something new every day. I felt it all in my heart. Although I may not have been able to express my happiness then, something wonderful and very different was happening.

The adults in our lives, out of fear, often tried to limit our scope, our potential for growth. Little White boys couldn't play with little Black kids. Christian White boys couldn't play with kids whose parents were hippies, or those who chose not to attend church. But when were left to our own devices, in a new environment that was pretty much a level playing field, we figured it out ourselves, and the result was bliss. No matter the ingredients in the stew, no matter what we threw in the pot, it tasted good. My brother and I were blessed, and we were experiencing a grand level of freedom.

Most of the time, we were truly cut off from America. There was no TV, and even the *Stars and Stripes* military newspaper was delivered two days late. It had to be shuttled into country by air from Vietnam. This was completely frustrating during the 1973 World Series between the Boston Red Sox and the Cincinnati Reds, the Big Red Machine, the best team ever in Major League Baseball, at least in my mind. Waiting an additional two days for baseball scores was torture. After all, this was my team: Bench, Rose, Morgan, Perez, Concepción, and on and on. Catcher Johnny Bench was the man, and I emulated him. One night, to aggravate me, Dad looked at a picture of Bench and went, "I am glad he can hit, because he surely is ugly."

"Ugly! You called Johnny Bench ugly?" To a ten-year-old, these were fighting words. But being cut off from "the world," as many called it, was hard. Still, we managed. After all, the pool, snack bar, and movie theater were open.

It became very apparent that we were going to enjoy a pampered existence while in-country. There was the outside world, where people sweat. And there was our world, comfortable and well fed. Who knows? Maybe because we were there to help the Thais defend themselves, in a portion of Asia that saw millions die in wars during the twentieth century, and to support the continued effort in Vietnam, we deserved the good life. Right? And we were eight thousand miles from home. Sure. But today I feel bad when I remember the faces of Thai children living in squalor. I remember being stared at through restaurant windows, trying to ignore the hungry faces. We moved from being poor Americans to being part of the nonexistent Thai middle class, and we were thriving. The thing that still makes me think, makes me sad, was that most of the world wasn't.

Because of a strong monarchy and a large, well-trained and equipped military supported by the US, Thailand had not seen the same issues that plagued North and South Vietnam, and later Burma or Cambodia, with the Khmer Rouge. Civil war, thanks to this tonic, did not happen in Thailand. The Thai monarch was adored. Every house had the king and his wife's picture available for all to see. It was against the law to disrespect the king and penalties were harsh. But the real pain, if you were dumb enough to disrespect the king, was from whatever Thai was in arm's reach of you. Disrespecting the king was a surefire way of getting one's ass kicked.

I saw a number of drunks get manhandled for getting a little too tipsy and running their mouths about the monarchy. The Thai New

Year was prime time for such events. Drunks roamed the streets, wandered into traffic, and put their hands on those they shouldn't. An ass whooping from a local bar owner was better than a trip to jail. The Bangkok police were ruthless, and you suffered greatly if you lost their respect. This was not the US where you got one free phone call and there was something called "due process." Thai police could lock you away anytime they wanted. Sometimes, civil order came with an iron fist.

Even with the strength of the monarchy, there was always internal political strife, which led us to our first challenge in our new home. Prime ministers and their governments were a dime a dozen in those days, which meant one day we woke up to a coup d'état. A radical student group demanding the overthrow of the current asshole in charge decided to seize several government buildings, some of which they torched. How Berkeley of them. But those poor misguided kids paid a heavy price for their mistakes—beatings, jail time, or worse.

The government responded swiftly and violently. From my hotel room, I watched buildings burning, tanks rolling through the streets, and helicopter gunships flying overhead. It was surreal. I watched this all unfold while on my bed, lying on my stomach, head cradled in my hands. Everything was safe on my side of the window. But on the other side of the glass was the Thai reality, which at that moment was hellish. I felt a great distance from the situation, almost like I was watching a movie on a big-screen TV.

For a while we were sequestered in the hotel and told not to venture around town. I think schools were closed. I remember Dad couldn't wear his uniform in public, so he would go to work in civilian clothes and change into uniform when there. One day, while hanging out being cool on the mezzanine, I thought the Thai guy who worked in the jewelry shop looked at me angrily and said, "I'm going to kill you!" Scared the hell out of me. I immediately went and got Dad to confront the guy. But it turned out to be quite embarrassing. He was scolding his younger brother for leaving the safety of the hotel. The guy was so embarrassed. I felt like an ass, but it was a nervous and scary time.

This was the duality of Bangkok. It could be wonderful, beautiful and fun, but at the flick of a switch, it could be cold and ugly and dangerous. We had been in-country for less than a month.

CHAPTER 5

Finding our Thai Home

Believe it or not, the hotel got old. I mean, how much baked Alaska can one eat? After a month or so, after surviving a hot LZ in Saigon and coup d'état in Bangkok, we needed normal. It had been about two months since I'd slept in a bed that I considered mine. We all yearned to find a house, move out of the hotel, and settle down, have a home-cooked meal.

The search for the proper dwelling was not easy. We looked at many before we all looked at one another and went, "Yep." We looked at townhouses in gated communities, apartments in ten-story buildings with pools, and traditional Thai houses. Most of them did not have air-conditioning, and the kitchens were normally separate from the house, with no modern appliances like refrigeration. They only had open-fire cooking and woks. Who knew how to do that? One place felt like we were in the middle of the jungle. Only God knows what would climb in your window there.

The parameters for the house really were simple: safe neighborhood, as nice as we could afford, and hopefully around other ex-pat families so Mark and I had folks to socialize with. No matter where we were in the city, the school bus would come to our door and shuttle us to school, so that was not a concern, but there was an American facility that we wanted access to called the Rec Center. It had an old golf driving range with a clubhouse and an Olympic-sized swimming pool that the Army had turned into a place for soldiers and their families to enjoy outdoor activities. It was on Soi 71, on the south side of the city, so our search centered on the area near the facility.

The cool thing was we could afford a lot more house than in the States. We settled on a three-bedroom, modern Thai-style house, on a little road off of Soi 71, about three miles from the Rec Center, called Soi Charanmit. As you approached the house, all you saw was a wall, about seven feet high, and a big electric gate that opened to a driveway. On top of the wall were glass spikes, kind of like a prison wall. We asked our landlord, a man named Kun Iyutt, why the glass was there, and he answered, "To keep *kamoy* out of the compound and the house." Kamoy is the Thai word for thief. That was eye-opening.

This type of protection was common. Driving down streets and alleyways, you would think there was no one living on either side. But on the other side of the walls, the world opened to you. As you drove through the gate, the house stood in front, but perpendicular to the main house was a corridor of rooms that were built in the old Thai style. There were three small bedrooms, and a washroom with a huge ceramic bowl that was used for bathing. There was also a traditional open-fire cooker. Kun Iyutt told us those were the servants' quarters.

Servants? We are going to have servants?

We learned it was common for ex-pat families, and Thai families with the means, to hire Thai women to be housemaids and cooks, and men to be gardeners. They would live either full-time or part-time in the quarters adjacent to the main house. This was mind boggling to me. I asked Mom and Dad how we could afford hiring maids and gardeners. Kun Iyutt said the average maid earned about forty dollars a month, or eight hundred baht in Thai currency. A gardener, because the job was part-time, would earn about half. The crazy thing was that those salaries were considered to be very good. It was surely enough to live well in Bangkok at the time. So, since we were paying them well, a living wage, it seemed okay.

The house was nicer than anything we ever had. In the corner of the yard was a small Buddhist temple, like the size of a case of beer on a pole. Kun Iyutt said it was a spirit house. Like kitchen witches in Belgium, or crosses in Christian homes, spirit houses are a Buddhist tradition designed to help keep the spirit world happy. The idea is that spirits lingering around your house will live in the spirit house rather than inside of yours.

The living room and dining room were one large room, and the walls were glass doors. You could open the walls and let air flow through, and there was a huge sliding door that went out to a patio on the front lawn. Full-length curtains allowed you to close things off and create privacy. Adjacent to the living and dining room area was a wet bar where Dad taught Mark and I to tend bar. (I learned to make a mean Harvey Wallbanger cocktail.) And there was an American-style kitchen, complete with a big refrigerator and a stove with an oven.

We learned immediately that we could not drink water that came from the tap. It was not potable. Water had to be purchased in big five-gallon drums and stored for consumption.

Let's break this down a little. The concept of running water in-house was relatively new to Thailand at that time. Only new houses had sewage and water. There was no purification available, so any pipe that ran to your house was basically bringing river water. It was clear most of the time, but the only things you could do with it was bathe, wash clothes, and clean the house. Drinking the stuff would be dangerous. And the concept of hot running water was extremely new. Each room, kitchen or bath, that required hot water had its own natural gas heater, which was kind of nice. You turned on the hot spigot, the heater turned on, and you had endless hot water.

So, we would buy big five-gallon containers of water and use them for drinking and cooking. We managed cold water by filling every empty container we had, soda or milk, with water and storing them in the refrigerator. Cold water was a luxury.

Stairs led up to a second floor where our bedrooms were arrayed. Along the stairs were large picture windows, and at the top a hallway that went from what was Mark's and my bedroom to a smaller middle bedroom, and then my parents' master bedroom. Mom and Dad's room was huge. It had a built-in office that looked out a large window, of course their own bath, a row of closets made in teak wood, and enough room for a sitting area. There was also a connecting door to the smaller middle bedroom, which became the nursery for my baby brother, Dan, who was born about a year after we got to the country. It was wonderful having a baby in the house. It really cemented us as a family.

Mark's and my room was great. We had our own beds, thank God for that, a desk for homework, and Dad gave us his old stereo so that we could play music and start to build an album collection. We put up posters and made it as cool as possible. We even had our own bath. This place was luxury.

Walking back toward the stairs, we noticed a door that went out onto a second-floor deck. It was our first look at the adjacent landscape, since the seven-foot wall obscured our view from the first. From the deck, we could see the many homes and apartment buildings surrounding us. Across the street was a marsh area of about three acres. Thais called marshes or swamps klongs. Behold, we were living next to a swamp, at least the remnants of one. With all the construction in the area, this was the one bit of land that could not be built upon, so it remained. What we didn't realize at the time was that all the wildlife in the area had been forcibly relocated to this one spot. Wildlife in Thailand is not furry and warm blooded; it normally has scales and cold blood.

The biggest surprise was that there were family homes on both sides of us, and one across the street. An even bigger surprise was that each had an American family, with a total of seventeen children, ranging in age from a few months old to eighteen. We had landed on American Ex-pat Island. Almost immediately, the families came out of their houses and began to greet us and introduce themselves.

The family in the house on one side were the Telfers. Father

Telfer was an Army lieutenant colonel in the Transportation Corps, and he worked at the Joint US Military Assistance Group (JUSMAG), Thailand, or JUSMAG-Thai for short. He wife, Hilthud, was a nice but strict German lady that he met and married while stationed in Europe. They had three sons. One was a year older than me and a bit of a bully. He was the kind of guy who would come over to your house to play, bring a big bag of potato chips, and not share. One time, Dad had gone up-country to one of the Special Forces camps in the north and came home with authentic camouflaged boonie hats for Mark and me, the ones Green Berets wore in the jungle. We loved our hats and wore them everywhere.

One day, the neighbor boy and I got into an argument, and he threatened to throw my hat in the klong. Words and threats got louder. He stole my hat off my head, ran into the street, and heaved it as far he could into the klong.

Now, let me tell something about klongs. No one in their right mind would venture into one of those things. There are weeds that to tangle your feet, weeds that stick and sting and burn skin. There is deep water, normally covered in green moss. The water just sits there and rots everything around them.

Then, there is a host of varmints: frogs and toads, some of them poisonous, mosquitos, bugs, walking catfish, fighting fish, and a whole assortment of tropical life. But by far the worse were a lethal assortment of snakes. We encountered poisonous snakes on many occasions, mostly scary cobras. King cobras, spitting cobras—the ones that spit venom into eyes and blind you—tree vipers, and a black-and-yellow striped thing that I couldn't identify. All were common in the klong, in the street, and in our yards.

So, my cool hat was gone, and I was furious. I went to Dad, who attempted to discuss the issue with Mr. Telfer, but to no avail. Some parents can never admit their kids are jerks. My parents were the first to accept our mistakes. Plus, Mr. Telfer outranked Dad, a military thing that's always in play. So, nothing came of the exchange.

I would get revenge another day. The hat sat deep in the klong, about thirty feet into the thick brush. I wasn't going to get it. Every day, I saw it sitting there, becoming sun drenched due to exposure and weaker due to rain.

The menacing Telfer and his two younger brothers had been friends. Except for the oldest, on occasion, they were nice kids. The one thing I will say about the older Telfer is he was very protective of his brothers. That was a good thing.

The Telfer house was beautiful. There was a large, open, formal living and dining room with two-story ceilings, a large bar next to the dining area, and a big room that was used as a family room with a console TV and stereo. We would hang out there and listen to music, watch TV, and dance. On the TV, we could get Japanese cartoons and movies with characters like Kamon Rider and Godzilla. Upstairs had three larger bedrooms that were all really nice, and a second-floor covered deck. It was pretty cool.

There was also a small front yard, but in the corner was a huge mound of dirt that turned out to be a red-ant mound. I made the mistake of jumping off a swing set seat onto the mound one day and was immediately covered in red ants. After finally getting all of them off me, I had thousands of little white bite marks all over my body. Thank God red ant bites only sting and are not poisonous.

The house to the other side of us was occupied by the Champlain family, a very large family that in many ways was like my dad's family. There were eight Champlain kids, more girls than boys. I remember the oldest girl getting ready to graduate high school and head back to the States. Dennis Champlain was the same age as my brother Mark and was a nice kid. He had an older brother who would pick on him at times. Dennis would cry, and I would feel sorry for him. His sister Denise hung out with us. She was cute and sweet.

There was always a lot of noise coming from the Champlain house. Like my dad's father, Mr. Champlain was a sergeant, and a bit gruff. We often heard him barking orders. Mrs. Champlain always looked like she was at her wits' end. The Champlains had an infant, too. Their house always seemed to be cluttered. In fact, I never went in, only seeing things from the front door. I bet the house was filled with constant motion.

Across the street were the Keeners. There were five of them. Father Keener was a big, tall, muscular guy, but he wasn't in the Army. His long hair was a key indication. In their yard, they hung a two-inch-thick rope at the top of a forty-foot coconut tree. Father Keener would climb the rope, hand over hand, no feet, to the top numerous times every day, or at least when he was around. He traveled a lot, and we eventually learned that he worked covert operations. I will not assume the agency or organization, but "black ops guy" was the scuttlebutt. Mrs. Keener was a really sweet lady and would wait patiently for Mr. Keener to return home. I remember their homecomings were always very passionate—like making-out-on-the-couch passionate. The Keener house too had glass walls. They were always welcoming, so our gang played at the Keeners often. They had a backyard that had to be half the size of a football field.

The Keeners had three children, two boys and a girl. The oldest boy, Jeff, was in high school. He didn't hang out with us much, but he was always nice. We heard through friends years later that he worked on fishing boats in Alaska during summers in college. He was the adventurous type and a bit odd. He wore overalls. Why? He also had a bowl haircut in the 1970s. Oh my God!

Matt was the second boy, and closer to my age. He was maybe two years older. We hung out a lot. Matt was cool and had many hobbies and fun things to play with. We would also travel around the city together, going to movies or shopping.

Many years later, I ran into Matt at Fort Benning, Georgia, at the Army Infantry School. Like me, he had become an infantry officer and completed a tour in Germany. We talked briefly and then went on our way. It felt kind of odd, considering we had been so close in the past.

Then there was Erin, a girl about Mark's age. Erin was sweet and cute and would play with the Champlain girls often. Rumor had it that Erin, after graduating high school, had moved to Japan to pursue a career as a model.

The Keeners had a dog named Pooch who was constantly in heat, like hump-your-leg in heat. Pooch was a mix between a boxer and a Labrador. The Keeners brought Pooch to Thailand from the States, so she wasn't a normal Thai street mutt. Pooch had a number of litters. We kids were allowed to watch Pooch give birth, and it was always fun to play with the puppies as they grew. One of the puppies became our dog, who we named Crash. Why Crash? He was clumsy and often ran into things. One day he went headfirst into the refrigerator, fell on his side, and went to sleep. What other name could have fit better? Concussion?

We all loved Crash. He resembled a small yellow Lab. We would play ball with him, and he would chase us around the yard. He was so much fun. The maids and gardener liked him too.

Life on our street was magical. Although we didn't see each other much at school, and we differed in age and grade, when we got home, we had this small and intimate community to enjoy. We would get off the school bus, say hello to Mom, and get a quick snack. Then we'd change from our school uniforms and were out the door to see what adventure we had in store that day. We played American sports: football, basketball, baseball. We would marshal all our plastic Army men and toy tanks and have a great battle in the Keeners' yard. We would all go to the corner candy store and get whatever Thai treat they had. One of our favorites was dried mango pieces, which resembled boogers, hence their name from that day forward. But we could also get candies from Japan that tasted nothing like anything we had in the States.

Another corner store sold Thai iced coffee and tea. Both were delicious, but I liked coffee the best. The shopkeeper would take a small plastic bag and fill it with shaved ice. Next, he would fill half of the bag with espresso-strength coffee and the second half with condensed sweet milk. A rubber band was tied onto the corner of the bag so you could hold it, a straw would finish off the presentation, and you were off. In two minutes, you were high as a kite on sugar and caffeine. Mom and Dad wondered why we were so energetic at the dinner table and had problems getting to sleep at night. After a few probing questions, they put a stop to the afternoon iced coffee habit.

The klong was a constant source of entertainment. During the rainy season, where we got at least an hour of pouring rain every day, the streets in our little hamlet would flood. Normally about six inches deep, yet with excessive rain, it could be as high as a foot to eighteen inches. Creatures from the klong would then venture into the streets. Amazingly, the streets would also fill with beautiful Thai fighting fish or betas, as called in most pet stores. We would spend hours catching fish and watching them fight one another. Of course, on occasion, we would run into something dangerous. One day, while reaching to catch a fish, a black-and-yellow snake emerged near the bank of the road and slithered between my legs, which scared the shit out of me. But it was still magic.

Snakes were common in the yard. One day, Mark and I were throwing the baseball back and forth, and movement caught my right eye. It was a baby frog being followed by a baby cobra, crown exposed. The cobra was looking for a meal. It was obvious that both were rookies at this game, but a cobra is a cobra, and at younger ages they are more poisonous. We did what we normally did: we got our gardener to get rid of the snake.

The gardeners would sell caught cobras to hospitals for the development of anti-venom vaccines. They could make a hundred baht for each foot in length. One day, we went over to the Keeners and their gardener had caught an eight-foot cobra and put it in the rabbit cage until he could get it to the hospital. While in the cage, the gardener had put a towel on the cobra's head so it couldn't see. But if you would go near the cage, the cobra would hiss, and cobras have a loud hiss. It had also chewed up the towel and saturated it with venom. We were all very happy when that thing was gone.

Rarely did we fight, but when we did, black eyes and bloody noses were common. One day, Matt Keener got into an argument with a guy who lived in another neighborhood. It was when we were riding the bus home from school. They decided to meet on a neutral street once we got home and settle things like men.

We all came together for the fight. Matt had his crew, and the other guy had his. It was like the scene from the movie *The Sandlot* where the two baseball teams meet to discuss the next day's game. Both sides exchanged insults, and then it was as if we were watching two English gentlemen discuss the Marquess of Queensbury rules before a prizefight. They discussed how the fight should proceed. "Come on, man. Just kick his ass."

Finally, they faced off. Both exchanged blows to the face and then quickly realized there were better things to do that day. Walking home, Matt cried. I had never seen him cry, but it wasn't because he was hurt. It was because he was ashamed of himself for doing something so ridiculous. He surely learned something that day. I think we all did.

It was best to play on our little island at night. It cooled off quite a bit, and often there was an evening breeze. We would have amazing games of hide and seek. I learned that I could hide in a garbage can if need be, to not be found. Winning was everything, and there was status in playing the game well.

Mark and I would come home filthy, and Mom would march us straight to the tub before dinner and bed. We were living a wonderful childhood, with a loving mother and father, and many friends on Soi Charanmit.

The Soi 71 Recreation Center was our American oasis. The Brits in town had their club where they watched cricket matches and drank gin and tonic. We had the Soi 71 Rec Center, where we could do American things: eat hotdogs and hamburgers, play baseball, basketball, and football, do cannonballs in the pool, play pinball, shoot pool, play tennis and racquetball badly, and listen to loud music. Basically, we would pretend we were home.

The Rec Center was only three or four miles from the house, so all we had to do was find a samlor or a taxi, pay them ten baht—fifty cents—and ten minutes later we were there. Summer days were spent at the Rec Center while Mom and Dad worked. All our needs were met. Friends from all over the city would meet us there for the day. In the evening, we either found transportation home in time for dinner, or Mom and Dad would meet us there. All you needed to get in was your military ID card, worth its weight in gold.

Mark and I played Little League Baseball at the Rec Center, and since it was always hot in Thailand, we played a couple seasons a year; in fact, play was year-round. In the evenings, when the adults who were our coaches got off work, we would have practice and games. The weekends were always a flurry of activity, too.

The first team I played for was coached by an old infantry sergeant who had done more than one tour in Vietnam. He treated us like soldiers, which wasn't the most motivating thing for an eleven-year-old. "I am going to run you until you drop. You will not quit. I will make you winners or die trying." Really? I think it's important to say that we didn't win, nor did we die. But I don't remember that season fondly.

The next season, I played on a team called the Reynolds Wraps, sponsored by Reynolds Aluminum Corporation, which had a headquarters in Bangkok. A "rap" was also getting a hit. An interesting play on words.

The first half of the season, we had a coach from Reynolds who just couldn't get us together. We went 3-3. At the season break, the coach announced that we couldn't stick around for the second half of the season, so my dad, who was a great pitcher in his day, and Chris Williams's dad took over as coaches. There was a reason Chris Williams was a badass, and one look at his dad made it all clear. His dad was tall and muscular like Chris, and a great athlete. He was soft spoken and a great coach, especially one-on-one. With their leadership, we started to hit the ball and score runs, win games. We were knocking the cover off the ball. Dad would pitch batting practice, which was key. Since he was a pitcher and had control, he could consistently throw strikes. To learn to hit, you need to know what a good pitch looks like. Dad could throw strikes, and so we learned.

Chris was our star pitcher on the field, and I caught like Johnny Bench—and more importantly, like Granddaddy. He could throw hard and fast, overwhelming most batters. I was pretty good behind the plate and could throw out runners attempting to steal. We had a girl playing first base. In the 1970s, this was a novelty, but she was awesome. Nothing got past her, and she could hit. Both she, Chris, and I became all-stars.

At the end of the second half of the season, we were undefeated and went to a championship game between the winners of the first half of the season, my sometimes ominous neighbor's team, coached by his dad, Mr. Tefler. Chris pitched. I caught. We hit the ball and scored runs. In short, we kicked their butt.

That day, I learned the meaning of the term schadenfreude—enjoying the misery of others. Considering it was my neighborhood nemesis, I decided to revel in it for a while.

Another part of life at the Rec Center was being a part of my dad's Army sports teams. Every military unit in town put together teams and competed in sports leagues, whether it was slow-pitch softball, fast pitch, or flag football. Dad always coached his unit teams, and they were always in the running for the top spots.

Teams from the US Army Communications Command, Thailand, or USACC-T, had many great athletes, and they won a lot. The teams really brought us together as a community. This was how families got to know one another and kids became friends.

Chris Williams's dad was assigned to USACC-T, as well as our sponsor Major Randy Richardson and his family, which included their sons, Darrel and Randy. We all became great friends. Mark and I would spend the night at their house, and then they would do the same at ours.

One of our favorite things to do was rat hunting. Rats in Bangkok were the size of cats and could easily scare dogs. We would take mop handles and tie nails to the ends, making a spear, and hunt at night. We would sit in ambush in the shadows of the outside buildings, and when we heard rats scurrying across the floor, we would turn on the light and attack.

The concept was ridiculous, and we normally screamed and ran away, but we should get points for trying. In case any animal rights organizations want to know, no rats were harmed during our clandestine activities.

Dad's commander was Colonel Sammy Cannon, a Texas Aggie and effective leader. Good commanders know how to motivate people. Colonel Cannon liked Dad and made sure he ran the unit sports program. He wanted his unit to win because he understood the effect winning had on his unit and the families of his soldiers. Winning was good for unit morale, esprit de corps, and brought the unit together. It made living eight thousand miles away from home a little easier.

Colonel Cannon did like his drink and, like Dad, normally scotch whiskey. For a short period, Colonel Cannon would have Dad and Major Richardson over to his quarters every night after work for a drink or three. In those days, when your commander invited you over for a drink, you went, and drank until the colonel was done. Dad started coming home three sheets to the wind, almost nightly, and Mom saw she had to put a stop to it.

In the Army, the only person with more power than the

commander is the commander's wife. Mom called Mrs. Cannon, asked for some help on the issue, and boom, Dad started coming home on time and sober as a judge.

The unit sports program introduced us to many wonderful people, like Captain Wes Green, who was a paratrooper like Dad, a Vietnam Sky Soldier, as well as the honor graduate of his Ranger School class, at age forty. He was a college athlete who still had all his skill when playing for USACC-T. Sadly, his marriage ended while in Bangkok, but he and Dad kept in touch over the years. He earned the rank of colonel before retiring and is happily remarried. Captain Green was cool. He would, and to this day every time he talks to my dad, say, "I still don't like White people." Dad just laughs, because he knows they both love each other.

My Grandmother (Amma) and Mom,
Richmond, 1944.

My Grandfather (Granddaddy)
shortly before his passing in 1970.

Mom around 1950.

Mom and Bobby, off to the Prom,
1960.

Granddaddy after the war, around 1950. Like me, he was well-fed.

Dad's graduation photo from East Tennessee State University, 1967.

My favorite picture of Mark, Mom and I, 1965.

Mark and I waiting for Santa, 1966.

Dad in Vietnam 1969, with 299th Combat Engineers. Making chow for the troops after a long period in the field.

Dad, Christmas 1969, with the 173rd Airborne Brigade.

Change of Command Ceremony, Headquarters and Alpha Company, 82nd Signal Battalion, Fort Bragg. We were leaving Fayetteville and after a short school in Georgia, Thailand was next stop.

Wedding day 5 February 1972, Fort Bragg.

Wedding day cake.

International School of Bangkok, 1974.

Holding brother Dan, 1974.

Brother Mark and I, Christmas 1975. Wow, had I changed...so had my behavior.

Mom and Iyutts   Mom, Dan, and Tasani

All five of us, post-Bangkok. We survived. It was 1979, at
Armed Forces Staff College in Norfolk. Mom, beautiful as
ever, was the center of our lives, and the strength. Little did
we know at the time, many years in Europe was in our future.

CHAPTER 6

International School

Our new school was the International School of Bangkok, or ISB. It was truly a step up and a different world. At the time, there were two schools that catered to the ex-pat population in the city. The first was Ramrudi International School, which taught a British curriculum. Most of the students there were either British or from countries that were part of the British Empire, like Australia, Canada, India, South Africa—in fact, many parts of Africa. ISB taught an American-centric curriculum, so the many American military kids went there. Other countries sent children there, too. With Bangkok as the capital city of Thailand, there were many embassies. As a result, we met kids from all over Southeast, Northern, and Southwest Asia, Europe, and Central and South America. It was amazing to see.

ISB had two campuses. The first, the Bangkapi campus, was in a beautiful neighborhood downtown, near the Asoke district of Bangkok, which now is very high end. Kindergarten through third grade was taught there as well as high school grades nine to twelve. This was where all the cool kids and prettiest girls were, and where all adolescent boys wanted to be.

Our campus was in the Bangsue district of the city, not so high end, so it was called ISB Bangsue. Just our luck, it meant daily rides on the superhighway. ISB Bangsue was about halfway to Don Muang airport. Although the campus itself was very nice, it was surrounded by slums. So when we were out in our gym uniforms, doing calisthenics and playing soccer or having an ice cream at the snack bar, we were being watched by children living in tin shacks. It was sad, but we were safe and unseeing in our bubble. Bangsue campus housed elementary grades four to six, and the junior high grades seven to nine.

Public schools in the American South had been basic, minimally funded, and designed to regulate the flow of working-age males into job markets. I think we often see such conditions in working-class communities where graduates' only hope is for a factory, coal mine, farming, or service-industry job. Then, of course, there's always the military option. The education system is thus designed to teach basic skills, ensuring a steady flow of graduates into economies with limited opportunity.

Education at ISB was designed to develop, stimulate creativity, and challenge students. Resources were plenty. Students were given more than adequate instruction and individual attention and guidance. The intent was for students to learn far beyond the basics, to develop into freethinkers. Many of the students we met from other countries were accustomed to this level of education. Their ability to think and flourish in such an academic environment was evident. Have a little fun with yourself and try to do math with a kid from South Korea, then discuss literature with a kid from France. It meant Mark and I had a lot of catching up to do.

When we arrived at ISB, I entered the fifth grade and Mark the fourth. Teaching was conducted in pods in large rooms, say forty by forty feet, with three teachers, each with a classroom area in one of three corners of the pod. The fourth corner was used for group activities. Pods usually had about sixty kids. Students would have a primary teacher, but for core subjects like math and language, students would go to the teacher that taught them at their academic level.

For example, I had high reading and math skills, so I went to the teacher that taught the advanced class for those subjects. I was average in writing and spelling, so I went to the appropriate teacher within the pod for those courses. It allowed students to always work at their maximum level. And this was neat: if you began to excel at a given level, you could advance to the higher-level class. Or you could regress to the lower level. But the environment was always positive and supportive.

The teachers were very good, and I remember many of them fondly. Mr. Lapine taught sixth grade and had a great manner with the kids. During lunch, he would gather together all the boys who were interested in American football and have us run pass patterns. He was a quarterback in college and had a great arm. He was also a great math teacher.

Mrs. Morton was my primary teacher in the sixth grade. She was tough and would make me stay in from recess when I didn't finish assignments. I remember one day she stormed onto a soccer field at lunchtime and marched me back into the classroom. I provided so many opportunities for my bros to laugh at me.

To be honest, my home life was so strict I used the classroom to push boundaries. I was often the class troublemaker. Mrs. Morton realized this and allowed me a little license, but only to a point. She never let me skimp on my academic responsibilities, and I am grateful for that. Like leaving the South and enduring the many shocks of life in Asia, moving from an animalist academic environment to one of abundance had its challenges. I was insecure in my abilities, so being the class clown shielded the chinks in my armor.

This was just the beginning of a litany of things my limited upbringing did not prepare me for, but I survived. I learned, and sometimes looked like a fool, but I adapted. This was a common theme throughout my life.

Mr. Izatt was a Scottish man who taught us physical education and was one of the most unique characters I have ever known. He always had a whistle to get our attention, but he would yell at us in his strong Scottish brogue. "Get over here, boy. Who do you think you are today? I'll kick your arse!" It's not commonly known, but under the Geneva Convention, Scottish men are allowed to curse, no matter the situation. They can't help it. It's genetic.

He really made us work out. He kicked our arses. Physical education in the South involved giving a group of students a ball and letting us chase it around a yard for an hour—no supervision, no instruction—while the coaches talked shit and smoked cigarettes.

Mr. Izzatt taught the technical skills of sports, and this concept followed us as we transitioned to junior high school. We learned the sports that the international community played: soccer or football, volleyball, field hockey, swimming. We had professional soccer players—from Scotland, of course—come and give us clinics. We learned the skills to play competitive volleyball. We learned how to serve, overhand and underhand. We learned how to set, overhand and underhand bumps. We learned how to spike, both back and front court. We learned the proper way to do things.

Field hockey is the most physically challenging sport I ever played. When having to run with the head of your stick inches above the ground, bent over at full stride, you develop muscles you never thought you had. I remember being exhausted and horribly sore after an hour of field hockey.

This was how all the different cultures blended. You want to get know a guy from India, play field hockey with him. We had art classes and lessons in the Thai language and culture. We learned how to live in the Thai culture and not get our asses kicked.

Do you know it is extremely insulting to point your feet at a Thai person? We learned not to do it in class. But this meant that you don't put your feet on furniture or on the back of a school bus seat. I learned that lesson the hard way after a very uncomfortable conversation one day with a bus driver.

We wore uniforms to school. The base rule was that all clothing had to be a solid color—white shirt, blue trousers, for example. This was where I was introduced to the safari suit. A safari suit kind of looks like jungle fatigues. There is an outer jacket-like garment with four cargo pockets in the front, not tucked into your trousers. Under the jacket, you wore a T-shirt. Trousers were the same color as the jacket. They kind of became the thing to wear.

Considering the cost of living in-country, we had our school uniforms tailored. When leaving the country in 1975, on my last day I rebelled and wore a pair of paisley trousers to school.

Intramural sports were a big deal. There were no other schools in town to compete against, so we competed against one another. The Brits at their school were too busy holding their noses in the air to tangle with us. We were all divided into sports houses: red, yellow, blue, and green. I was in yellow house and proudly wore my colors during physical education and sporting events. We would play intramural sports at lunch and after school. It was a lot of fun. We played international sports at school and American sports at the Rec Center.

Playing sports was a highlight of my time in Thailand, but I enjoyed being a "cool guy" even more and wanted to do cool things. Of course, we cool guys had a fight song. I can't remember the official school song, but I do remember the unofficial one that we "cool guys" loved to scream at the top of our lungs. It starts,

> Hidie hidie, Christ all mighty, who the hell are we?
> Zim Zam, God damn, we're from ISB.
> We're Colonel Tucker's motherfuckers, raiders of the night!
> Zim Zam, God damn, rather fuck than fight.
> Going down Soi Asoke, looking for a whore . . .

You get the idea.

As one can tell from the ridiculous lyrics, it was sung by prepubescent males who had no idea of the ways of fornication, nor were they properly equipped. I can only assume the more explicit pieces were from watching dogs fornicate. All dogs had more experience than us. But screw it; we were cool and we knew it. The girls around us must have thought we were idiots.

This leads us to our first lesson in Thai language and culture. As stated earlier, cussing is a basic skill for young falong boy, so repeat after me:

Yet ma! Translation: Go fuck your mother.

Quay suk! Translation: Suck my dick.

Mi me samong! Translation: You have no brains.

Pop quiz: Put all three into a cohesive verbal exchange.

Answer: Yet ma! Quay suk! Mi me samong!

Excellent, A+. Just remember, these phrases may get your ass kicked. I was hanging out with a group of guys who were starting, and I emphasize starting, to grow up, mature—at least physically. We were noticing and beginning to desire girls. Our daily conversation included girls, sports, girls, sports, nude girls, sports, sex with girls, sports, and which of the girls at school we fancied. It was constant, and girl stuff became more and more a portion of the banter.

I had many bros. Some were American with military fathers; some were American ex-pats who had lived in-country all their lives. Their parents worked for the US embassy, corporate or private businesses, or government activities that operated under a covert veil. We won't talk about them. And there were kids from other countries whose parents had an equally complex list of occupations. The thing was, we all had the same interests, so all the different cultures were seamless. Culture, race, ethnicity was respected, but in the eyes of a group of preteen boys, none of it mattered. We all looked at and treated each other the same—like horny dogs.

Coming from the South, where the color of one's skin was the litmus test of how you were treated, to a society where none of that mattered was the most freeing thing I had ever felt. It was even more beautiful to see Black men, women, and children—marginalized while living in America—free and happy. We were free to see and treat everyone based on the things that truly mattered: how good they were at sports, whether they were a deadeye at marbles, or if they could pick up chicks.

Now I know why Black soldiers get out of the Army in Germany and stay there. They are free, and they aren't judged the same way they are in this country. One of the best and most talented people I have ever known did this. He learned German while on active duty and had a family. After his first marriage ended, he met a woman from Sweden, followed her there, learned the language, and created a family business. He's the richest man I know, and he came from nothing in this country—from the poorest area of Atlanta. I love you, Manuel Knight. We went to combat together, and he will always be my brother.

There were many social activities, associated both with the school and the Army, which created opportunities for young people to meet and interface, potentially verbally and physically. The school had numerous dances throughout the school year, often in the gymnasium, and the Army had a teen club on Soi 21. There were dances with live bands every weekend. It was hard to find a dark corner in the gymnasium at school, but the teen club was like a nightclub, with a large bandstand, huge dance floor, and couches placed in comfortable sitting areas, all basically in the dark. The only thing that lit the place was a disco ball and numerous black lights, the ones that made posters glow. You know, the ones you used to stare at after smoking . . . sorry, story for another time.

We were basically a bunch of dorks hanging out at dances. My friend Mike Wright and a host of others would join us on occasion. Mike's father was a White guy from California, and his mom was Mexican. He was chubby with long, straight black hair, and stood maybe five two. He was the guy who always wanted to dress cool; bell-bottom jeans and platform shoes were the rage. Then he would do his best to bird-dog chicks, which he sucked at.

One night, I wanted to dress cool, so Mike let me borrow a pair of platforms. It was evident immediately that I did not have the balance to pull it off. More importantly, the platforms clashed with the straight-leg tan jeans I had on and my T-shirt with a cowboy on it. My mom was still buying my clothes, so sneakers went back on.

His father owned a restaurant on Sukumvit Road called the Cock and Bull. It was a cool little place. You could go there, have dinner and drinks, and then Mr. Wright played English- speaking movies. The place was always full of ex-pats.

Nothing frightened or intimidated Mike. If he wanted a cigarette, he had a cigarette. If he wanted a beer—in Thailand, there was no drinking age—Mike had a goddamn beer. Mike enjoyed trying to get me to do these things. Sometimes he succeeded, sometimes not.

We would go to the snack bar at the teen club, grab a couple of burgers, and try to make eye contact with girls who wanted nothing to do with us. Dances basically involved us sitting in the corner, too repulsive to be taken seriously by a girl, with everyone else on the planet laughing and dancing . . . until one night.

The band that night was pretty darn good. The club could hire a Thai cover band for next to nothing, and these guys were killing it, playing one great song after another. Bad Company, Led Zeppelin, the Stones, Gordon Lightfoot—yeah, Gordon; I said it. The band started playing "Sundown," a slow song of his that was very famous at the time. All of a sudden, a girl, who was probably a ninth grader— yes, an older woman—asked me to slow dance. I nodded, and we walked on the floor. Mike's face turned either white in fear or green in envy. I couldn't tell; the black light changed everything. He sat and just stared at us. I felt kind of bad for him.

Blood was pumping so fast through my veins that I thought I was walking on air. I couldn't feel my legs. She turned to me and we came together. We swayed and circled around the dance floor, not saying a word.

"Hi," I finally said.

She said, "Hi" back.

"I'm Mike. Thanks for asking me to dance."

She smiled. I felt I had to talk, but words came hard. Every time I attempted conversation, she would smile and then look away, almost as if she was bored. I was at the pleasure of whatever my female master wished.

At the end of the song, nothing was said, but I had danced, and it was a slow dance with a girl! My life changed forever. The next song was fast, "Bad Time" by Grand Funk Railroad. The same girl and I made eye contact, and we approached each other to dance. Now, slow dancing is easy, basically a moving hug. Fast dancing takes some thought and coordination, both of which I lacked at the moment. I just started swinging my arms and moving my hips and trying to keep time with the music. I had watched *American Bandstand*, and even better, *Soul Train*. I had an idea of what to do, if only I could relax enough. As I danced, I overcame my fear.

The girl had a smirk that said, "What the fuck are you doing?" We kept on dancing. My bros were hooting me on in dark nether regions of couch city. Again, at the end of the song, nothing was shared other than a glance and a smile. But that night, I transitioned from being repulsive to going out dancing with chicks. "Hey, see you next weekend, babe."

Everything changed after that night. At school, I was getting information from my bros that girls were taking notice of me. In fact, a girl named Chris Hunt "liked" me. Chris was cute, tall, and slim, with curly brown hair, and the gods of puberty had blessed her. I was a decent athlete and occasionally hung out with sports buddies who had girlfriends. Chris Williams had a girl, and her best friend was . . . guess who? Chris Hunt.

Chris Williams was hands down the coolest guy in school. His dad was Army and worked with my dad, so we had chances to see each other outside of school. Chris was the guy that everyone wanted to hang out with. He was a muscular, tall Black guy, and the best athlete in the school. We had many good athletes at ISB. Chris also wore a perfect Afro, the coolest haircut ever. Girls loved him. Chris told me that I could go out with Chris Hunt if I wanted. I thought about it a little and decided to give it a go.

So, the plan was for me, Chris, and his girlfriend, Kelly Parker, to meet Chris Hunt at a local bowling alley, to see if I had enough game to pull it all together. We bowled. We did stupid things to try and make the girls laugh. Chris Hunt and I made eye contact and quickly looked away. We bowled some more. We ate food and told dumb jokes. At the end of the date, we all went our separate ways. I told Dad that I thought Chris Hunt and I were "going out" but I wasn't positive. He asked me when we were getting married and laughed. I got embarrassed and went to my room.

The next week at school, I learned from a reputable source that my new heartthrob was no longer interested, and that was that. But I still felt like I had accomplished something—a real date. The school, my friends, my budding social status, were all moving in a good direction. Life was really changing, and I was a happy kid. I couldn't remember feeling that way in a long time.

CHAPTER 7

Out and Around Town

You must taste as much of the culture as you can when living in a foreign country. We didn't spend all our time inside our safe spaces at home, school, or the Rec Center. We spent a lot of time venturing into the Thai world.

The use of samlor and taxis became second nature and made travel within the city very easy. For years, we kids would roam the city freely, using any method available. Can you imagine parents allowing their children to do these things today? samlor and taxi ride costs were negotiated, and of course drivers, when seeing young falong boys, would double the price. We had to be good in our negotiation skills. Most ride costs could be cut in half from the initial offer. Some negotiations did not work out, so I was glad to have considerable Thai cursing skills. Most of the time, a few choice phases were exchanged, and the driver would flip us off as he drove away. On occasion, he would hop outside of his vehicle, promising an ass whooping if we didn't just go away.

Riding in samlor and taxis always reminded me of the James Bond movie *Man with the Golden Gun* as much of the movie was shot in Thailand. One of the scenes showed a few flashes of a Thai taxi driver cursing at traffic problems—traffic made by James, of course. We saw this movie in the theater, and it was funny to see how Thais in the audience reacted to the agitated taxi driver. They all burst into laughter. Of course, they knew what was being said, and the actor in the scene was a famous Thai.

Another scene in that movie took place at a Muay Thai match, Thai boxing. Dennis and Darlene Champlain were extras in that scene, and for a brief second you could see them cheering in the stands.

We took buses only if we were broke. I think it was a dime or two baht to go anywhere on a bus. Riding the bus was safest in the evenings; the rush was during the day. So, occasionally we hopped on a bus to get us from one end of Sukumvit Road to the other, which was a good seven miles or so.

Bus drivers never hesitated to stop and kick off a bunch of falong boys who were misbehaving. One night, a group of us took the bus from Soi 21 to Soi 71, fifty blocks—at least that was the plan. A friend of ours could make the weirdest squeaking sound with his voice, almost like a whistle, and very loudly. He started squeaking at people walking down the street, freaking them out. People would react like a gun just went off. We thought it was hysterical. After about three times, the bus driver lost his patience and invited us to leave. It was a long walk home.

Street food was amazingly good, but potentially dangerous. Western immune systems are not developed for all the culinary challenges in Southeast Asia. Guys on bicycle carts would drive through the streets selling stuff ,and people would set up food stalls on the side of the road. You could feed yourself very cheaply.

My favorite was a noodle soup that the Thais called *whitial nom* (noodles and water). It was very similar to Vietnamese pho, but with Thai spices. It was delicious, filled with amazing broth, any size noodle you wanted, fish balls that were really good, fresh vegetables, beef, chicken, tripe. You could get your order to go in a plastic bag, or vendors would serve you in a bowl at their stand and chat with you while you ate. The problem was how the bowls and spoons you used were washed. After a dine-in meal one day, we saw one vendor's method for cleaning his spoon was to run it through his mouth. It was at that point that Mom put a stop to the practice of after-school whitial nom. Damn. We still snuck some in on occasion in plastic bags, when she wasn't around. The soup was so good that at age twelve we happily took our chances with communicable disease.

These days, you can find Vietnamese pho everywhere. And when I go to Thai restaurants, I'll ask if they can make whitial. When living in Virginia in the early 2000s, I found a restaurant that would make it just for me. I would get a couple of orders of Thai spring rolls, and a bowl of nom. I was a happy man. It's funny what stays with you for your entire life. The spices, smells, and flavors always take me back.

Fruit is one of the most unique and delicious types of food of Thailand—creamy, sweet, and just amazing. One fruit, called durian, smells like sewage, but if you can fight your way past the smell, the taste is wonderful. Hold your nose. Markets are open all the time, but mostly people frequent them at night when it's cooler. They are amazing social events. Couples and families stroll through the markets, eat dinner, buy produce for the next day. It is such a beautiful scene, and so many of the foods are truly unique. Food is the backbone of the culture. Because of their abundance of agriculture, Thailand is one of a handful of food-exporting countries around the globe.

Another favorite was an ice cream treat that probably would not translate to American palates. A vendor would take a hot-dog-like bun, sweet bread, place either a fruit-like jam or sweet, sticky rice on the bottom of the bun, then place scoops of a gelato-like ice cream along the top of the bun. It was happy days when the ice cream dude showed up. Sad days were when we had no cash, or he didn't show. On a hundred-degree day, this was heaven on a bun. The flavors of ice cream were unique. One of our favorites was vinegar.

Going out with Mom and Dad was also at a different level. Best thing, we didn't have to ride a samlor or taxi. Dad bought a powder-blue Ford Pinto station wagon that we tooled around town in.

Now, I think it is only honest to remind you that this man initially showed up driving a new Chevy Corvette. He then traded it in for a Chevrolet Impala that rivaled the *Titanic* in size, and now he relegated himself to a powder-blue Ford Pinto station wagon. Let's take a moment and dissect this. Powder blue is, next to pink, the most effeminate color ever. Secondly, Ford Pinto. At this moment in history, US automakers were dropping the ball. After making some of the best cars in history, like the Mustang, the Shelby Cobra, the '57 Chevy—American muscle—they were making garbage. The Pinto was probably on or near the top of the shit list.

The engine was so anemic that when you turned on the air conditioner, the car slowed by ten miles per hour. It was like Dad had tapped the brakes. Lastly, station wagon; my poor father had finally donated all his manhood to his family. I guess we should be grateful, but let's be honest, it was a little embarrassing. He must have gotten a hell of a deal on this thing. Happily, when we left country, we sold the car, and some other poor bastard got to exhibit his diminishing testosterone levels in the thing.

Back to dining out and going out in Bangkok. Even then, Bangkok was a city of the world. The city had an economy that could meet any taste. Today, it rivals any city in the world. There is true affluence, and Thais live in a thriving economy. One day, I will return. I want to see everything again, especially ICONSIAM, Bangkok skyscrapers, Koh Samui, and Chiang Mai. I also want to see all the places of my childhood—Pattaya, Sattahip, Ayutthaya.

The first indoor mall I ever saw was in downtown Bangkok. It was where I bought my first rock albums. One day, Mark and I went there and found a record store. So cool! We shopped for a bit, and then I found two albums that I thought I would give a go. I had no idea what I was buying, but they turned out to be two of the best albums of their time, by one of the most influential bands of the era—Bad Company. I had already heard a few of their songs—"Ready for Love," for example—but knew nothing more. So,

I decided to buy their first album *Bad Co.* and their second, *Straight Shooter*. Both albums have become classics. They cost a hundred baht a piece, or five US dollars, which was a ton of money to the average Thai, especially Thai kids running around in the street. For some reason, I had the two hundred baht in my pocket. Happily, I paid the cashier and walked out of the store, and into mall traffic.

Little did I know, two Thai kids about Mark and my ages were watching us in the store as we purchased the albums. When we left the store, they followed. Soon, they were harassing me, thankfully not Mark. After all, I was carrying a package of new records.

I assumed one was going to try and get my attention while the other tried to snatch my albums or make a go for my wallet, which was now empty. One of them would walk by quickly, bump into me, and then cross in front while the other followed, waiting for the right time to pounce. Once I figured out what was going on, as the kid made his bump and run for the third time, I stepped on one of his flip-flops as he passed. His momentum made him walk out of his shoe. As he did, I picked it up and tossed it across the mall. I braced for a fight, but fortunately, the kids ran for his shoe rather than coming at me with fists and feet. It gave me time to blend into the crowd and get outside, never to be found. I have often wondered why his shoe was more important.

Movie theaters were probably our most current connection to happenings in the rest of the world. We spent many hot afternoons and evenings there. We saw *The Sound of Music, Patton*, and several Bruce Lee movies. But James Bond was the man. We saw both Sean Connery and Roger Moore on the big screen. Bond films were hugely popular with Thais.

Theaters were palaces. The price of a seat differed depending on seat location and size. Seats on the lower level next to the screen were ten baht, or fifty cents. A little farther back were the twenty-baht seats, or one dollar. Then, there were the balconies. For fifty baht, you could sit elevated, with a perfect view, in a huge reclining seat with waiter service, all at the touch of a button. The button would summon a waiter who would take your order and bring you anything you asked for: soda, candy, popcorn. So neat! I used to love Fanta Cola—no redeeming nutritional value at all, but, boy, was it good! There were three flavors I remember: red (I think they were trying to mimic strawberry), yellow, which was logically lemon, and green. I had no idea what flavor they were trying to reproduce there. Any Fanta hit the spot on a hot day—cold, wet, tons of sugar.

Our favorite place to eat was a restaurant called the Carlton. Imagine walking into a Humphrey Bogart movie like *Casablanca*. Dark, smoky room—everyone smoked then and could legally do it inside—and tables with white linen tablecloths, candles in the middle, waiters in white tuxedos. Grand piano in the corner, with a tip vase on top. It was like walking into a place in the 1930s or '40s. I always wondered where the Nazis were hiding. But the main thing I remember about the Carlton was the food.

In this restaurant, to this day, I had the best meal of my life. Now, I am not trying to disrespect my grandmother, or my wife or mother, but the truth is the truth—the Carlton wins. I have dined all over Europe, the best cities in the US and the Middle East, but nothing matches.

The dish that did it was a platter, not a plate, with five rock lobster tails arrayed from left to right. Most restaurants will bring you a two-pound lobster. Maybe. But five tails in the same meal? That's insane. And it was deliciously cooked in butter and broiled to perfection. The lobster was so good that I don't remember the side dishes. Who cares?

One night at the Carlton, Mom and Dad were having dinner without us, and Dad choked on a piece of rock lobster tail meat. He almost suffocated. Mom was too small to get her arms around him to do the Heimlich maneuver. Luckily, a doctor was in the restaurant and saved Dad's life. Scary stuff; the best dining of my life almost killed Dad.

Mom and Dad used to frequent another place called Nick's Number 1. They took me and Mark there once, but it was a distant second to the Carlton. I pray it is still there.

This was Bangkok. This was how we lived. We could afford to have our clothing and shoes for school tailored. We could afford to have furniture custom made for our house. We could afford world-class cuisine. Would I ever again be so spoiled?

Dad grew up with very little, and to see him able to do things for us and himself was beautiful. As the PX system in South Vietnam started to draw down, they would ship goods to the PX in Bangkok. The prices were ridiculously low. Dad bought a nice stereo for the house. He had a Sansui four-channel receiver and dual turntable and an Akai four-channel reel-to-reel tape deck, plus four big Sansui speakers. We could have never dreamed of having something so nice in North Carolina. We didn't know such things existed. So, for all of us, it was a true revelation. It started a passion in me that I have maintained through the years. I often buy vintage gear to have around the house. I think old-school stuff sounds better than new, but it also reminds me of those halcyon days, filled with music, in Bangkok.

As I've said before, there is a duality to life in Asia. So far, I've told you of the most beautiful parts of life there. Thankfully, the beautiful side was more common that the ugly. But Bangkok could be dangerous . . . very dangerous. We spent a lot of evenings out in the community. We liked to bowl, and in the city, there were many world-class bowling alleys, which seemed the size of airplane hangars. One of the places we frequented had fifty-two lanes. I don't think I have ever seen one so big since. Inside, they were shiny and new. The lanes were perfect and the seating areas modern and cool. There was more than one snack bar, a bar, and many other areas to socialize.

Americans and Thais filled these places. One night, my parents were bowling in an American military league at one end of the complex. The remainder of the place was filled to the brim with Thais, laughing, drinking, bowling, having the time of their lives.

Thais love to party. There were many common libations on the Thai bar menu, but common folk drank beer like Singha and Amaret, and they drank a local whiskey called Mekong. The Mekong River is one of the largest rivers in the country, and Bangkok sits at its southernmost delta, joined by the Choa Pyra. Mekong whiskey was obviously named after the river, and the whiskey looked like river water. It was scary stuff. I remember it being strong and spicy. The spice was probably added to hide the taste of formaldehyde. Although I knew nothing of whiskey at the time, I remember it burning as it went down. I recently bought a bottle at local liquor store, but I just can't find the courage to open it and give it a try. Only God knows what would happen. I'd probably get arrested for streaking around the neighborhood.

But Mekong was the basis for Thai bartending in the city. If you weren't sitting in a plush hotel with a bar that sported Scottish, Irish, American, Japanese, Indian, or Mexican whiskeys, your whiskey sour was made with Mekong.

In the middle of the alley, a group of men were swilling beer and Mekong. They drank consistently during the night and got progressively louder. From the outside, they appeared to be a bunch of friends having fun, men and women having a fun evening out, until . . .

I was sitting down at the long bench that sectioned off the two lanes my parents were using. We were surrounded by friends. No one was drinking, at least not heavily. But the place got rowdy. Suddenly, out of the corner of my left eye I saw a shiny flash. As I turned to look, I saw a young Thai man pointing a nickel-plated .38 special revolver at the head of another Thai man. Then three shots rang through the cavernous room, each entering the body of the unfortunate man. Thankfully, there were other people in my view, so I did not see the bullets penetrate the man, but I clearly saw the gun fire and recoil, and the shooter aim and fire again and again. Time slowed to a crawl.

Women screamed. My dad yelled, "Everyone get down!" He grabbed my mother and moved her to safety, then looked for me and Mark. In the hysteria, people panicked and screamed. I watched the gunman run out the exit door at the far end of the alley.

Smoke hovered over the lifeless body as the smell of gun powder filled the space. It is a smell I have hated my entire life, even after being in the Army. It was mayhem for a few moments. And the reaction was far different than what would have been experienced in the US.

In the US, no one would have touched the body. In Bangkok, they immediately started to reposition the body, and finally someone who worked at the alley brought out a sheet and covered the dead man. The carpet was soaked in blood.

Next, US the cops would have showed up quickly, and they would have wanted to question as many people as possible to see what they could learn about the incident. It took the Thai cops what seemed like an hour to get there. During this time, a covered, dead body was lying on the ground, and people were looking at it and chatting.

Lastly, and this is the craziest thing I think I have ever seen, everyone eventually went back to bowling and drinking and having fun. This included all the Americans at the far end of the alley. I couldn't believe it. It was like everyone was just stepping over the family dog lying on the living room floor.

My brother Mark thought he would leave our safe corner of the alley and sneak a peek at the body. Dad, seeing him inch towards it, went and retrieved him. He got really upset at Mark. I think he even smacked Mark on the noggin. He wasn't angry at Mark; he was afraid for him. Dad acted like a soldier under fire. Adrenaline was rushing through his veins. Dad saw a lot of combat in Vietnam, and more importantly, he saw the effect of combat on the human being.

I too have seen what guns do to bodies, and it's horrible. To this day, despite all my military experience, and knowing that a gun in the house is likely the best way to protect my family, I still can't own one. I served in units that lived with their weapons, slept with them.

But in my home, around my children, I just can't. Dad didn't want Mark to see the results. The adrenaline was in control. He knew it would scar him for the rest of his life. I didn't see the bullets pierce the poor dead man, but the image of the gun firing over and over will be etched in my mind forever.

Whenever I have a conversation with someone about our time in Bangkok, after the surprise and some nice stories, this one always comes into mind. I struggle a little to determine if I should start to paint the dark side of life there, because it will always change the mood. Sometimes I go dark, sometimes I don't.

The cops finally showed up and took the body. The gunman was probably never found and brought to justice. Bangkok and the surrounding jungle made it easy to hide or disappear. The gunman could have been hiding anywhere, and the gun was probably at the bottom of some klong or river. The odds are, he got away with it. I often wonder how a society can be so distant, so emotionally uninvolved with their fellow man, that moments after seeing a murder, they just ease back into their daily routine. It was obvious no one really gave a shit, or maybe spectators were conditioned to such violence.

I remember feeling like I was in a dream. I was frightened, and adrenaline was pulsing through my body. I huddled at the end of the cold, plastic bench that sectioned off the area where my parents continued to bowl. I shivered as I sat there, and stared at the bowling pins, watching them fall and then be reset by the machine. I didn't want to look towards the body. I didn't want to see it, and didn't want the same treatment from Dad that Mark had gotten. I just wanted to go home.

CHAPTER 8

Venturing Outside the City

Bangkok was a bustling metropolis, and as I said before, today it is one of the largest and busiest cities on the planet. Back then, when driving outside the city, things became very simple very quickly. It was like the city was a huge island in the middle of nowhere, and when you left, you immediately plunged into the depths of a green ocean. You literally went from concrete, heat, and dust to pristine earth and countryside. After months in the city, sometimes the quiet was too much to bear.

Farms lined narrow, two-way roads. People lived with less than their compatriots in the city, and at a much slower pace. It was peaceful and beautiful. Electricity was a luxury, and things like air-conditioning were almost nonexistent. This made the people strong and resilient. They seemed smaller and more fit than many in the city. Their skin was darker and hardened by the sun. They worked every day. Most were fishermen, farmers, or street vendors of some sort.

You saw small businesses, but none with major reach. A small corner store was basically the extent of services to an entire community. Occasionally, you would see a Mekong bar or a brothel, or a sign for Fanta or Singha beer. Picture the movie *Platoon*. That was life outside Bangkok.

Our landlords, Kun Iyutt and his wife, would often take us into the interior of the country. Both Mr. and Mrs. Iyutt were graduates of Cornell University. They were intellectuals, part of the upper class, and we were happy that they took an interest in educating us about Thai culture. After all, the countryside was still the heart of the nation at that time, not its few cities.

We rode elephants. We saw Thai boxing matches. We saw traditional Thai dancing and theater. We also went to a crocodile farm, and it was a bit overwhelming. I don't like snakes, and I dislike alligators and crocodiles equally. There were thousands of these creatures, all staring at you like you were lunch. Men would do things with these creatures to make your skin crawl. After finishing with the crocs, Kun Iyutt made sure a great restaurant was on the agenda. It was so much better to have lunch than to be lunch.

This was the splendor of the Thai countryside. One restaurant turned out to be a shack on the side of a klong. It served fish caught daily from the klong. The food was delicious. Most restaurants served fish that had been out of water at least a few days. At this place, they would catch, cook, and serve within minutes. At first, we were taken aback, but after we sat down and had the food, we began to enjoy the beauty of the place. It was the first restaurant where I had freshwater mussels. The cook fire-roasted them, placing them in shell on a grill top. The fire would cook them, and the shells would open. The smoke and fire gave them a wonderful flavor. I can still remember how the char on the shell added flavor to the mussel. Amazing.

They brought a huge bowl of seafood stew to the table, full of any form of creature that swam in Thai waters, all delicious. It was the first time we saw an octopus. As we were digging through the stew, a small one floated to the top of the bowl. We all looked at each other, wondering who would go for it. We had only seen these creatures on TV, never face-to-face. As we debated who would give it a go, Mark snatched it out of the pot and popped it in his mouth. We were all impressed. He said it was salty and chewy. But it showed you shouldn't judge a situation too early, because the simplicity of the place was no indication of the wonderful food and the atmosphere. It was about opening your mind. My friends from northern US states often laugh when I say the best barbeque in Alabama is normally found at a gas station. They just arrogantly laugh. One day, I will show them.

We even ventured out to meet Aswan's father at his country house south of the city. Aswan was a good man, but he was another example of the quality of people we associated with during our time in country. He was well educated, having attended university in the United Kingdom as well as in the United States. Remember, Dad met him at a professional military school. Countries only sent their finest to those things. Aswan was the true example of a professional military officer.

His father's country house was a simple dwelling raised above the water level by stilts. The walls of the house would open to let air move freely through the dwelling, and there was a covered patio, also on stilts, where we met.

He was a very nice man, and we learned that he was also a general in the Royal Thai Army. Aswan was following in Dad's footsteps. I always find it interesting that most countries I visit have families with a tradition of military service. Thailand certainly had one. The profession of arms is not one for amateurs or those faint of heart. We learned that he played an important role during the coup d'état we experienced when first getting to Thailand.

Thailand is known for hundreds of miles of pristine coastlines and some of the most beautiful beaches in the world. Today, these are tourist havens. When I retire, the first thing I want to do is visit Koh Samui and Koh Phangan islands. Forty years ago, these places were simple and clean, safe, with no sign of the corporate world. One of our favorite places to vacation was Camp Samison, which was an Army post on the Gulf of Thailand. Although there was an ongoing military mission there supporting operations in Vietnam, and by that I mean an adjacent B-52 base, the place was an oasis for people wanting a break from the craziness of Bangkok. Families could rent villas next to the sea for next to nothing, and just relax. Mark and I rented bikes and traveled anywhere on post we wanted.

It was one of the greatest times of my young life. We felt so free.

There was a nightly outdoor theater that showed current movies, and an officers' club on top of a hill with a perfect view of the gulf. They served traditional American food. It was the place I first had creamed beef on toast—or as it is called in the Army, "shit on the shingle." All I remember is stuffing my mouth with the stuff and wiping gravy from my face.

The beach at Samison was pristine, and it seemed like no one was ever on it. It was never crowded during the day. Maybe people who were assigned there were too busy listening to the enemy or strapping bombs to B-52 underbellies. Today, beaches like these are covered in intoxicated foreign tourists. Forty years ago, you couldn't find a single footprint in the sand.

Picture the Camp Samison beach; on the far left was the officers' club on the hill, and as you looked from left to right, there was, white untouched sand and crystal-clear water. It ended hundreds of yards away at another untouched hill. We were in our own little cove. The skies were always cloudless, blue, pollution-free. We would pack a cooler with drinks, fill a picnic basket, and spend the day on the sand.

One day, I chose to venture alone away from the group. I took a fishing rod and walked what seemed like a mile away from our camp and just spent some time alone. I walked into the waist-deep water and hurled my baited hook out and stood there, looking around our little paradise. I was alone in God's perfect creation. It was one of the most peaceful, beautiful, and surreal moments of my life. I was alone, but it was okay. I was not afraid, confident in myself. It was as if I were in the hands of God. It was the perfect moment.

I caught a little yellow fish that day, removed the hook, and let him go about his business. He didn't seem upset; after all, I provided him with lunch. That day I learned that I need time alone, solitude. It's where I find the greatest peace and do my best thinking.

Pattaya Beach, one of the most famous places on the Gulf of Thailand, was another place we enjoyed. Like Samison, the beach forty years ago comprised a series of wooden huts, a few bars, and the occasional hotel. People would sleep on the beach and enjoy the pristine water.

Dad's roommate from Fort Bragg, Dan McKinney, was stationed at Pattaya. He was an army Special Forces officer, and his current assignment was running the 1st Special Forces Scuba School there. Rough duty. We would visit him and his wife and sleep in their very traditional Thai villa.

Uncle Dan, as we called him, would give us blow-dart guns and have us patrol the perimeter. I don't remember what the hell we were looking for, but it was so the adults could party in peace. The secret to a blowgun is to breathe in your air before you put your lips on the gun. If you don't, you could taste the dart as you are digging it out of your throat.

To operate the scuba school, Uncle Dan had to purchase services from Thai fishermen with big boats. He would take us out on these things that looked like Chinese junks and teach us scuba and snorkeling. Mom and Dad would lash on scuba gear and give it a go, and Mark and I would grab a mask and snorkel and swim around the boat. The water was so warm and clear.

On one trip home after a weekend in Pattaya, we took a chartered bus. The roads in the country, even in town, were a tight two lanes at best. Imagine a bus and a large cargo truck trying to share the road, at speed.

I was sitting next to the window, about five rows back from the driver. I really could not see forward. I wasn't tall enough at the time. But as the bus approached a bridge, I was told, a cargo truck approached from the other direction. Considering the brain trust that normally drove these things, normal behavior for the driver of the cargo truck would be to accelerate, determined to win the race over the bridge. What he didn't calculate was the bus was moving too fast and was too heavy to stop before both vehicles arrived at the bridge, at the same time. Ain't physics a bitch?

Everyone who could see this situation develop suddenly screamed and gasped in fear. But somehow, as the two vehicles passed, the bus driver did something godlike, preventing a crash. Maybe there were angels present. In a matter of a few seconds, this man maintained his composure and skillfully guided this large craft filled with human souls and barely missed the oncoming cargo truck. He saved all our lives that day.

Everyone cheered and thanked him. Many were in tears. I wondered why he was looking so pale. As I digested what had happened, I thought how crazy it would be to not see death coming, for it to come so unexpectedly and fast. This bus driver deserved sainthood, having saved forty lives that day.

One summer, I spent a week at a Boy Scout Camp at Pattaya Beach. The camp was down a dirt road, about two miles from the main part of town, so basically, we were in the jungle. The camp had a number of World War II–like barracks, an old Army-style mess hall, and a long pier that jutted at least fifty yards into the water.

It was a magical week, but considering all the Boy Scout leaders were military, they ran the camp like a military base. Reveille woke us up at 0600 hours. We immediately washed ourselves, made our beds, and cleaned the barracks. Breakfast formation around the flagpole, every troop in military formation, was at 0700 hours. The head scoutmaster would call us to attention, our individual scout leaders would offer our report, number of people present, number absent, number on sick call. No one ever went absent or to sick call. Then, the national anthem was played as we saluted the flag. After honors to the nation, we were released to march to the mess hall, for an orderly breakfast.

After breakfast, everyone went to classes, all of which they had chosen—sailing, swimming, arts and crafts, archery, you name it. Formations were held three times a day—breakfast, lunch, and dinner. At lunch, scoutmasters gave announcements and handed out mail. Announcements always included the results of the morning barracks inspection. Mom sent me a letter each day, and I could tell she was always crying. We didn't like being apart.

The cleanest barracks were always celebrated, giving the winners bragging rights for the remainder of the day. Screw 'em. It's important to note that me and my group were the camp slobs, never winning the daily inspection. We really didn't give a shit. But days were spent doing really fun stuff in the sun and jungles of paradise. It was a pretty good deal.

At night, we would play rousing games of capture the flag, basically teaching adolescent youth paramilitary skills, like how to execute a tactical raid, conduct a hasty defense, and, occasionally, hand-to-hand combat. It was fun, but can you imagine two hundred kids running around in a jungle in the middle of the night? Can you imagine being a scoutmaster and having to account for all the kids doing that? I am amazed everyone made it home alive.

We had a camp song, and it was ridiculous, but here it goes:

Around a campfire and under a tree.
The Gulley Gator, he said to me.
Who would want you, I would like to know.
'Cause every time I see your face, it makes me want to go . . .

You sang, screamed, this verse over and over, until someone made you stop . . . thank God. Now, I have no idea what a gulley gator is. I'm not sure I want to know.

All told, the Boy Scouts in Thailand were amazing. Our troop, number 702, was formed by 1st Special Forces Group, so in celebration of this, we wore the green beret. Very cool. Being a scout in Thailand was not like being a scout in the States. It was a ticket to travel all over the country and see things that tourist dream of—well, maybe.

We would camp in the oddest of places. Near the Burmese border, about three hours northwest of Bangkok, was a place called Arawan Falls, a mountainous area in thick jungle with falls in full force during the rainy season. To get to them, you had to hike up a steep path, and as you got closer you could pick areas with pools to swim in and enjoy the cold water falling on you.

Pools at lower levels were normally full of people escaping the heat, but the higher you climbed, the more privacy you were rewarded. We decided to hike as far as the heat would allow us one hot day, finally reaching an empty pool. We hopped in, and I can still feel the cold mountain water on my body. The pool was deep. No one could touch bottom. Dense jungle canopy protected us from the sun, and the water quenched our bodies. It was a magical experience.

There was a cleared field near the falls where we camped. We arrived close to dusk one evening, so we immediately pitched tents and started to cook. This is where I learned how to cook on an open fire. We made rice in a pot on the fire. Spam was a normal protein source we would take camping, and it was a pretty good in combination with the rice and some fresh mango.

When we awoke the next morning, to our surprise a herd of water buffalo had surrounded the camp. Water buffalo are about the size of a VW microbus, so they could have trampled our camp with little effort. But we coexisted peacefully. They occupied one side of the field, we the other. The hardest thing in dealing with the average water buffalo is flatulence. First, water buffalo dung is the size of a pumpkin—huge and mushy. Never step on or trip over one; chances are you will lose a shoe. And secondly, their farts come often and are extremely loud. I mean, car-horn loud. At least you had a warning. Other than that, they made for nice neighbors.

The best place we traveled to was the town of Ayutthaya, which sounds like "I-yute-tee-ya." To get there, we would hop a train in Bangkok and ride north for a few hours. Train travel in Thailand at that time was very basic. There were no air-conditioned cars, no place to buy food. You had to either carry your own or buy from street vendors. Seats were wooden benches, and cars were filthy. Crowding was never a problem, but, as you might guess, this was not the Orient Express. After a few hours of being jostled around by the train, sweating profusely, we would get off in Ayutthaya and step into a new world.

It was like a town in the American West in the 1800s. The roads were dirt, and dust flew everywhere. Open-floor row-house dwellings lined the streets, and open-air markets were the only economic activity. Vendors selling fruit, candy, and Fanta would swarm as you got off the train.

When camping, I would carry Dad's field gear from Vietnam: a medium rucksack, his mummy sleeping bag, food, water in his plastic canteen, and some basic clothing. If I had ammo, it would be combat load, but for a twelve-year-old boy, it was pretty heavy.

One trip, the plan was to camp at a "scout camp" near the Choa Prya River, about two miles outside of town. We asked for directions to get there, and all we got was "That road, two miles, on the left." We humped our gear down the dirt road in sweltering heat, and after two miles . . . nothing. We dropped our gear and started to look around, finally finding the camp. From the road, we could barely see a few wooden A-frame structures about four hundred yards off the beaten trail, with no obvious path leading to them. Trails, if any, had been covered with jungle. But we all carried machetes and hacked our way to the camp.

When we arrived at the A-frames, it was like the ground was moving. Snakes using the buildings for warmth scurried out of the area. They illustrated why our training was essential. First thing you do is make a fire. You want to have light. Without it you become prey. Then you clear as much brush as you can. Easier to see the enemy coming. Then you cook, and then prepare for sleep.

We managed to get the through the night with no hassle. Luckily, the A-frames were intact, and screens protected us from bugs and things larger and more deadly. Still, it was an interesting twenty-four hours. In those situations, you learn how strong you are and you realize what you can endure. Yes, there was wildlife and things that could hurt you, but most wildlife wants nothing to do with man. We slept, cooked, ate, and then went on our way. This was how you camped in the Boys Scouts when your adult scout leader did two tours in Vietnam.

The best trip to Ayutthaya involved hiking the famous *Bridge over the River Qwai* trail that memorialized all the US and British prisoners of war who died during the building of the bridge and railway. Their Japanese captors were brutal and unforgiving. In the movie, of course, the bridge was made from wood, the only readily available material. Thankfully, the Allies successfully destroyed it in the final scene. Remember Alex Guinness getting shot and falling in the river, then his lifeless body floating downstream? It was a great ending to a great movie. So, we were going to cross the newly built bridge along the railway that those heroes had built. Hundreds, if not thousands, died. Our mission that day was to cross the bridge and then hike to a cemetery filled with the graves of these men, about three miles. Good thing the bridge was rebuilt using iron, for now the Thais used the railway and the bridge for commerce. It looked just like the bridge in the movie, though.

As we started our hike, we formed a long line, a column, and started the crossing one by one. This meant walking on the tracks. There was no sidewalk. There was no safety net below to catch you. If you lost your balance, the river stopped you. It was scary trying to concentrate on walking on railway tiles, having to look down and see the river a hundred feet below.

Foot traffic on the bridge made the crossing even more harrowing. Vendors carrying their wears would almost push you off the railing as they passed. They did this every day, and no falong boy was going to slow them down. The column moved along slowly. The bravest of us went first. Others lagged and remained close to our scout leader, who took last position to try and account for everyone, shouting instructions to those struggling ahead.

Halfway across the bridge, the worst of all possibilities happened. A train arrived, coming from behind. Oddly, the Thais on the bridge did not panic, but they did pick up the pace. Along the bridge, there were a few places where you could get off the rails and escape the oncoming train, kind of like observation posts. We saw one about two-thirds of the way to land and beat feet as fast as we could to get there. As we drew near, we saw something we could have never imagined.

In this little observation post was a man with leprosy. The leper was lying on the floor of the post, taking up much of the space. As we arrived, we saw the man and froze. This was when panic began. The man was in the late stages of the disease, having no fingers or toes. His nose was gone, and there were sores all over his body. He struggled to lift his head as he stared at us. We stared back, wondering what to do. This memory always reminds me of the movie *Papillion* where Steve McQueen visits a leper colony after escaping a French prison. He goes into a hut and meets the head leper who offers a hit from his cigar. Steve takes a long drag and gives it back.

The leper asks, "How do you know I have dry leprosy? We learn that wet leprosy is contagious, and dry is not."

Steve replies, "I didn't."

Well, we didn't know the difference as we stood there staring, and the train kept a rolling.

The truth is, we really didn't know until afterward what this person was, what he was dying from. All we knew was we were scared and had to act. We had to make a fast decision. In a split second, we all ran toward land. One fear overtook the other as we kept on moving and finally made it. It's amazing how if you act, you can overcome fear. My therapist wife told me this was trauma. I don't know. I feel it didn't harm me. I feel it made me stronger. Like the godlike bus driver, I didn't let fear take over. You act and hope for the best, which is better than dying in place like a coward.

As the column crossed the bridge, we all gathered around each other, covered in sweat and hunched over, trying to catch our breath. After all the excitement and running with rucksacks on our backs, we made it. We all overcame our fear. It just goes to show, when you think you have Thailand figured out, you learn very quickly that you don't, kind of like life.

We finally regained our composure, drank a little water, and moved on. We headed to our campsite for the night, adjacent to the cemetery. It was reported to be haunted, but we were too exhausted to be worried about ghosts. We had hiked a good four miles in the jungle, carrying everything we needed to survive. We camped at the cemetery gate. I pitched my dad's shelter half and rolled out his down-filled mummy sleeping bag. That night we ate C-rations, the old Army field rations, and they were actually really good. I bet most people these days have no idea how to use a P-38, the small can openers that came with C-rations. We drank hot canteen water that smelled and tasted like plastic, but we didn't care.

We talked and sang songs, and then went to bed. I remember sweating like a hog in Dad's sleeping bag; it was rated to keep you warm at twenty below. As I fell asleep, I thought about the man on the bridge. Yes, he was a man. Leprosy was his disease. I hope he was fed and had a safe place to sleep. He is always one of the people I think about when I think of Thailand.

Even with all the drama and physical exertion of the day, we were happy, and sleep came easy that night.

CHAPTER 9

Poor Decisions, Bad Behavior

If you've read this far, it may be obvious that you are reading a coming-of-age memoir. The stories so far may seem a bit intense, and perhaps unique. Not everyone is witness to a murder, or a person dying from a horrific disease while a train approaches on a bridge. This chapter, however, is different. It involves three stories that I'm not necessarily proud of. I have often debated whether to share them. They all involve poor decisions and accompanying bad behavior.

I finally concluded that although I do get to choose the stories I tell, I should have the moral courage to talk about personal issues that may not be flattering. So, here we go.

As we approached our teen years, Mark and I became increasingly interested in social acceptance, being part of the group. We wanted to be cool, and girls, girls, girls were our primary motivation.

My crazy group of friends were more willing to try things, push boundaries, and do things that would surely get us in trouble with our parents. These things were necessary for social stature, or so we thought. With our environment being Bangkok, there was no social restraint on anything we wanted to try. In the States, there were rules galore. Our parents were overflowing with rules. Bangkok had no rules, and if we could figure out how to maneuver under the parenting radar, the possibilities were endless. There was no drinking age, no smoking age, and no limitations as to how deep you wanted to dive into the underworld cesspool that thrived in this city.

I had my first cigarette when I was twelve. One evening, Chris Williams, Mike Wright, a couple other dudes and I found ourselves at a dance at ISB, Bangkapi, the high school campus downtown. Bangkapi was one of the most affluent areas of town.

Dances for junior high kids were cool, at least to us. Everyone wanted to dance, and dancing meant you were cool. It meant you had matured beyond simple childhood, into the world of girls.

Dances at the high school, however, were basically launching platforms for activities during the remainder of the evening. "Where's the party?" People would show up to dances, find their friends, solidify plans, and then "blow this popsicle stand" or "make like a tree and leave."

At one point, more people were leaving the dance than hanging out. So, we did the cool thing; we started to follow the crowd. Kids had congregated on the street outside the campus gate, and many of them were smoking and chatting. Me, Chris, Mike, and the rest of our clan went down the street about a hundred yards and stopped in the middle of the street to talk. As we gathered, Mike, always the instigator, presented the group with a pack of cigarettes. "You guys want one?"

I just looked at the pack. Now, my parents and grandparents smoked. The first thing Amma did in the morning was sit down at the kitchen table, pour a cup of coffee, overflow the cup with condensed milk for some reason, and then light a cigarette. It was the daily routine. Granddaddy smoked cigars and chewed tobacco, sometimes at the same time. It was common for both of my parents to have a cigarette in their hands. The house was always filled with smoke. They smoked at meals, while they tended to my baby brother, Dan, while driving and shaving. It was like a cigarette was a permanent appendage. Considering they were doing everything single handed, it took some skill. It was kind of impressive to watch someone manage a lit cigarette while feeding a baby. But until this moment on that Bangkok street, I had never considered smoking.

I hated the way it smelled. Have you ever had someone take a bite of your food and exhale smoke all over it? Makes me want to vomit. Dad loved to ask for a bite of my sandwich.

I did not want a cigarette, but everyone in the group immediately pulled one from the pack and lifted it to their mouths, waiting for a light. Welcome to the world of peer pressure. Finally, I gave in.

We looked so stupid. We were still in elementary school, looked and dressed the part, and were standing in the middle of the road with unlit Marlboro cigarettes hanging from our lips.

The lighter started to make its rounds. Mike, then Chris, the other dudes, then it was my turn. This wasn't a game of spin the bottle like in the hotel. I couldn't run away and meekly reenter the circle. This was something I had to do to be cool, to be part of the group, to make girls notice me.

So, the flame met the end of my cigarette, the tobacco lit, and for the first time, I drew smoke into my body. I still remember how good it tasted. I remember the sound of tobacco burning. The gross smell that I hated was gone, and it was actually pleasant when I inhaled the smoke.

It was apparent that others in my group of misfits had done this before. They would take long drags and suck the smoke deep into their lungs. One of them warned me about inhaling. "Be careful at first, man. Inhaling burns." So, I took smoke into my mouth only, careful to not inhale. It did burn, but I thought I did okay for my first time. The others laughed at me for being such a novice. I didn't care. I had one too, so fuck off.

We formed a line abreast and started to march back to the group of high school kids lingering in the road, all of us puffing away. One of the guys in the group would take a hit, and as he exhaled, he would say, "I'm cool, man!" Others did the same, and ultimately, so did I.

What a schmuck.

As we arrived at the center of activity, no one paid attention to us. Even at the nucleus of the atom, we were still negatively charged electrons, rotating around the core, not allowed to enter. It was still okay. Together as friends, we were cool. We hopped on a samlor and rode home, smoking the entire way. When I got home, Mom looked at me funny, like I smelled bad. I wonder why. Maybe I was a little high.

When the word gets out that you're cool, opportunities come your way. "I hear you smoke. Want to go outside and burn one?" Almost everywhere I went from that day on, people were offering me smokes.

As a father, I have tried very hard to effectively guide my children through these sorts of issues. I wanted them to enjoy alcohol but have a healthy relationship with it. Like Dad, I believe that smoking is the most dangerous thing you can do to yourself, and a long list of my dead family members is the proof. Sex, well, that's a hard thing to discuss, especially with daughters. I guess I should be happy that the boys don't have a brothel available to them. In short, we all make our decisions and live with any consequence. I hope I have helped them make better decisions than I did.

One day at the Rec Center, a guy on my baseball team indicated he had a pack and asked if I would like to go out to the far baseball field, sit on the bleachers, and smoke. We both took cans of 7-Up out in the midday sun, lit up, and enjoyed a nicotine and sugar break. Sadly, this was becoming a routine. I eventually started to inhale smoke and therefore began to ingest nicotine. I found out that nicotine makes you a little high, and I started to enjoy the buzz. This was becoming a problem, a habit.

It got to the point where I was hiding cigarettes in my room. The habit was becoming so consuming that in the evenings after dinner, I would try and find a place to hide and sneak in one or two. I would go outside our gate into the street and light up. I would go out on the upper deck, sit down next to the privacy wall so I couldn't be seen, and smoke. I became so brazen I would lock myself in my bathroom and smoke. It was getting out of control, and I was becoming addicted at age twelve.

One night, our next-door neighbor Mr. Telfer saw me smoking in the bathroom. There were two large windows in the shower, and he could see me from his upper deck. I was stupid. I was staring into my mirror and taking long deep drags, and watching the smoke exit my body. Mr. Telfer did what any good father would have done: he told Dad, and thank God for that. I look back on this and wonder how my life would have turned out if I had kept smoking. Tobacco has not been kind to my family. Uncle Leroy, Amma's brother, died of lung cancer. Amma died of emphysema, and what a miserable way to go. When she died, she had less than 10 percent of her lung function. Although Mom and Dad both quit smoking in 1980, she was diagnosed with lung cancer that spread and ended up all over her body, killing her. Little did I know it that night, but my smoking days were over. Today I am grateful. I have even found out that most of my biological father's family died early of cancer. They all smoked and drank heavily.

Dad, in short order, found my smokes. I knew something was up when I went for a nightly smoke and the pack was gone. He didn't approach the subject directly. He asked me probing questions, wanting me to confess and tell him the truth. We played cat-and-mouse for a few days, until I broke.

Let's be honest, all of his waking life was spent with a cigarette in hand, so how could he berate or punish me for smoking? For Mark, Dan, and I to be engulfed in cigarette smoke all day, every day, was not healthy. Considering that, the only logic behind the bull approach would have been "I am your father, I am the boss and bigger and stronger than you, so do as I say, or I'll kick your ass. Hold on while I light another nail."

Dad realized the duality of the situation and approached it far more fairly. I even realized how hypocritical that approach would have been. If he had been mean about it, I probably would have continued to smoke to spite him.

We talked sincerely. We sat in our living room. He said that if he could stop, he would. He realized how addicted he was. He talked about smoking being unhealthy and dirty, and that it would kill him if I smoked and got sick. He appealed to me as his son, not as a kid that broke the rules. I was really scared when the conversation began, and it took me a little while to realize he was trying to talk to me as a young adult. Maybe he realized I was beginning to grow up and how crazy the young adult social scene was in Bangkok. Eventually, I relaxed and began to talk with him. "Dad, I just want to be liked."

At one point in the conversation, he said he wanted me to eat a pack of cigarettes as punishment. When he was younger, he was caught smoking and had to answer to his father. Eating a pack of cigarettes was his father's solution, and Dad finally realized as he sat next to me with a cigarette in his hand that it didn't work. If anything, it made him resent his father more. Thankfully, I did not have to eat cigarettes, but the exchange will be burned into my brain forever. I found a new respect for him that day.

I guess he felt I wouldn't learn or act without punishment. This is when I realized that he didn't really know how to handle the situation. He was grasping for an answer. I think for the first time, I saw frailty in him. God knows, there have been millions of times when this was true about me and my kids. You want to do the right thing but aren't sure what it is.

"You are a good athlete, you have friends at school, and everyone I work with says what a great kid you are. You don't need cigarettes to be accepted. I love you, son. I don't want you to suffer, now or many years from now. I know you could continue to smoke, but I want you to look me in the eye and make me a promise. I want you to promise to stop."

I said I would. He hugged me. I have to say, I was overwhelmed.

Most of these interactions involved physical acts, fear, pain. Normally, I was spanked. This time was different. It was so important, it had to be different.

He asked me to quit. No, he told me to, but then trusted that I would. I promised him I would stop, and to this day I have not had another cigarette.

Although I truly have not smoked since 1975, alcohol has remained an issue in my life. As I write this, the issue is under control, but there have been times where it has not been, like after my mother died, or when stationed overseas in combat units. It would have been best if I never started with such things.

We merry band of misfits began to experiment with alcohol, another commodity readily available to anyone with the money to purchase, age irrelevant. There were several bars around town that ISB students frequented. The most popular was a place called Pop Shop. It was nestled down an alleyway off Soi 21, also called Soi Asoke.

Pop Shop was a small place, but very hip. The bar was closed off, had an actual door, so it was air-conditioned. When you walked in, the bar on the left along a wall sat perpendicular to the door, with about six stools. Behind the bar were built-in shelves that held whiskey, mainly Mekong, and a stereo. The bartender at Pop Shop always had cool music playing, and could make any Mekong drink, which was basically changing any commonly known name to a Thai-sounding one, like whiskey sour to Mekong sour. He could serve a mean cold beer, Singha or Amaret. These two breweries competed for top dog when we were there. They were both horrible, watery, and weak. Singha has surely taken a top position in recent years, exporting their product globally. I have no idea if Amaret still exists.

Across from the bar, on the right side, a series of small tables sat flush along the wall, each surrounded by chairs. Maximum capacity in this place was maybe thirty. At the far end of the bar was a jukebox and a small dance area.

The place was dimly lit, mainly by black light, and posters of bands and those crazy psychedelic ones covered almost every inch of wall space. Above the dance floor was a bedroom, which could be used by those who had activities other than drinking on their minds. The wildest thing was a window in the bedroom that was opened to the main bar, giving everyone present a view of all activities going on upstairs.

It was insane. People would sit and drink and watch the window like most people would sit and drink and watch a ball game at a sports bar. This was surely one of the craziest things I ever saw.

Occasionally, we would show up and see what was happening at Pop's. Mike Wright would order a drink called a J-Bomb. I have no idea what it was made of, although Mekong surely was in there. I would usually opt for a Mekong sour. It tasted like lemonade, and there was no hint of alcohol. Dangerous. One night, we walked in, and there was a soldier that worked for my dad sitting at the bar.

"Holy shit!"

He was sitting in the middle of the bar, drinking with a few high school kids. When we made eye contact, I told Mike that I had to get out of there fast, and we left. We regrouped outside the bar, and the soldier casually followed a few minutes later. I assumed it was to give us the indication that he knew it was me, or maybe he was as nervous as I was.

Like the cigarettes incident, I thought I was dead, for sure. But nothing came of it, and I have often wondered why. Maybe it was because he was hanging out with high school kids, teenagers, drinking alcohol with minors. This could get him in major trouble with the Army, so he kept his mouth shut. Or worse, and I think this was the right answer, this guy was selling drugs to kids.

My dad's unit had more than one soldier get into trouble for using drugs. They also had a few who were convicted and sent to a Thai prison for selling them. No matter his reason, the soldier decided to keep his mouth shut. At least, neither Mom nor Dad ever approached me about the incident. There were times when I felt like they knew something but chose not to say anything. At this point, we were coming to end of our tour in-country, so maybe they just opted to handle the situation by moving us back to the States, where these type of things were not possible for a twelve-year-old. Who knows?

Another ISB bar sat on a corner of Sukumvit Road. One night, Mike and I went in for beers and pizza. For some reason, Mike always drank beer with a straw. That night we both got straws and started to suck down cold beer. It took all the flavor out and made it too carbonated.

In the booth next to us, a high school guy said, "You know you are drinking with kids from the junior high school when they drink their beer with a straw." Funny guy, but the joke was on him. We were still in sixth grade.

Suddenly, a Thai woman in her twenties started to chat me up. I mean, she sat next to me in the booth, pressing her body against mine, trying to get something going. I know that she was a lady of the evening. Bangkok was full of them, but why in the hell would she focus on me when there were obviously older, more capable guys in the bar?

Mike and I had a few sips of beer and then decided to go elsewhere. As we walked out of the bar, this woman followed and tried to get us to spend some time with her.

At that moment, we were too young to know how sad and potentially dangerous this incident was. This woman was probably forced into prostitution. And what I learned years later was that families would sell their daughters into that world. So, this poor woman was just trying to survive, and I was a target of opportunity.

Who really knows what was in store for us if we had followed her into a dark alley. Human trafficking was real then like it is now, and there was always a market for young boys. God only knows what could have happened to Mike and me that night.

Our adventures into alcohol wasn't limited to trips to local bars. It transitioned to drinking together at home when parents weren't around. One week at school, four of us planned on a sleepover the coming weekend. Our friend Jeff was going to host, since his parents were going to be out of town. We planned and schemed for the event all week, bragging to whoever would listen that it was going to be a huge party.

We all got permission from our parents, and then the big party was on. We took samlors to Jeff's apartment around noon. The place was grand and very large. The floors were all done in granite tile, and a deep balcony ran from one length of the place to the other. There was a beautiful pool for us to use and plenty of food. For some reason, I don't remember any of the house staff being present that night. I assume Jeff gave them the night off.

When we got there, the afternoon started innocently, with food and music and a lot of shit-talking. After lunch, we went for a swim. Then Jeff pointed us to the bar and a refrigerator full of Singha beer in quart-size bottles. We each grabbed one and started to chug. I realized I liked the taste of beer—when not coming through a straw. We drank and drank.

All of us started to feel woozy. I was surely getting drunk. In fact, I was getting really drunk. I finished the bottle and started to act like an idiot. Everything was hysterically funny. I liked drinking. I liked being drunk. This was the most fun I had ever had—until the room started to spin, and my stomach started to turn, and I was barfing my guts out in a bathroom.

It was one of those type of hurl matches when everything comes up and then you start to dry heave. Goodbye lunch, goodbye Singha beer. I was shit-faced. I had progressed from taking a few sips of a drink at Pop Shop to drinking beer for the effect of alcohol. Just like the cigarettes that progressed to inhaling and then needing a nightly smoke. I was out of control.

After my dry heaves ended, I was useless. My head and stomach hated me, and all I wanted to do was sleep it off. As day turned into night, and I had some time to nap, then eat and rehydrate, I started to feel better, somewhat at least. This is when the boys told me of the plan they derived while I slept it off: Patpong.

I went, "Patpong?!"

Like Forty-Second Street in New York during the 1970s and the Las Vegas Strip of the same period, Patpong was famous for, well, a certain form of entertainment. Of course, Forty-Second Street and the Vegas Strip have since seen rebirths that made them family-centric tourist meccas. I've learned that Patpong is still the place you go for a "quickie" or maybe an "all-nighty." It depends largely on your wallet.

We band of idiots wanted to go to a "whorehouse," as we called it, and of course, Mike Wright knew just the one. With a whole lot of skepticism, we hopped on a samlor and rolled into the heart of the city. It's important to note, at this moment in my life, I had not been fully blessed by the gods of puberty, and was not necessarily ready for this form of activity physically. Nor was I prepared from an emotional perspective.

It was becoming clear that I needed to distance myself from my band of misfits that were now becoming idiots. Even at this age, I wanted any sort of activity with a girl to be intimate and special. Paying a woman thirty baht—yes a mere dollar and fifty cents—for a quick shag I was not prepared for was crazy.

Not to condone any of this, or my ultimate behavior regarding this situation, but I think it is obvious that Thai culture views sex far differently from puritans in the States. Sex to them is more like cable TV. Everyone has it, and it's something you do for fun and to relax in the evenings. It's not this holy venture, blessed by the gods. Therefore, it's important to note that all such activities in Patpong were legal. I got in the samlor.

Soon, we arrived in Patpong, where there were lights, loud

music, girls, and those suspected of being girls walking the street. Men roamed like prides of lions on the hunt. Mike led us down an alley, to a place with a metal door. He rapped on it a few times. A guy opened the door, the security dude, and let us in.

We walked down a dark hallway to where a woman stood at an open door that opened to a large, well-lit room. In the room was a set of bleachers, like the ones you sit on at football or baseball games. On the bleachers sat many young women, all scantily clad, each wearing a numbered button.

The lady who met us at the door led us into the room and asked each of us to pick a number. You were supposed to select the woman you wanted.

As we band of idiots walked in the room, every woman on the bleachers started to giggle. Shit, I wonder why. We each picked our new "friend," who reluctantly left the bleacher and took her new friend by the hand and led him upstairs. As we walked up the stairs, the lady would drop her cover, exposing her backside. It was quite a surprise, but I have to say, even today, nice touch!

My friend took me to her room. It was small and barely large enough for a double bed. The walls were made of plywood. Essentially, we were in one portion of a larger hooker cubicle farm. There was a hole cut in the plywood so you could voyeur the activity next door. It was dark and sparse, and one could only imagine the required penicillin shots afterward.

She left the room for a few moments and then returned wrapped in a sarong, a cloth wrap, commonly worn by both men and women. She closed the door and then dropped the sarong, exposing her body. She then lay on the bed and motioned me to join her.

I needed to be in proper uniform, so I slowly began to remove my clothes. Shoes, socks, shirt, pants . . . underwear. It was the moment of the great reveal. As I dropped trou, she looked down and giggled. Not so great for my confidence. As stated, I was still quite physically unprepared. However, seeing a slim, young nude woman had at least resulted in a proper physical response. I stood there nude with my hairless penis, not much larger than a Vienna sausage, at full attention.

The sex really wasn't sex. She guided me through the act. I guess I should be grateful for that. There was no penetration. I was allowed to fondle certain important parts of her body, and after a couple minutes, she ended things. I got up and sat at the end of the bed. She wrapped herself in her sarong, and as she left, she patted me on the head and looked at me with pity—or disgust. Probably a bit of both.

The band of idiots regrouped in the alley and decided to call it an evening. Low on money, we took the bus home. I remember we sat next to each other and didn't talk. We got back to Jeff's apartment and crashed.

The next morning, I borrowed money from Jeff and hopped a samlor home. I was tired and just wanted to be home, in my own bed. But more so, I just wanted to be a kid again. I wanted to be safe in our little hamlet of ex-pats.

Our adventures into the adult world showed us we weren't ready. It didn't taste good and caused you to feel like shit afterward. And it could be dangerous. We had dipped our toes too far into shark-infested waters. From that moment on, the band of idiots saw less of each other. We had run our course.

As I live with these mistakes in my mature life, at times I am sad and sorely disappointed in myself. Taking chances like these affected my life. I often wonder what it would have been like to fall in love in high school or college and if my first sexual experience had been special. Stupidly going to Patpong ruined that for me.

CHAPTER 10

Maids, Gardeners, and Aswan

Having outsiders like maids and gardeners—people foreign to you in more ways than just culture—living in your home takes real adjustment. Most came with references and recommendations, normally a good word from another family as they departed the country, but that was all we knew about these people. There was no way to conduct a background check, and we had several helpers rotate through our house, then leave for various reasons—school, wedding plans, just tired of the work, or sick of the pain-in-the-ass kid who lived in the bedroom upstairs. It was agreed by most of our help that I was "difficult." I simply felt that disciplining the oldest son wasn't part of anyone's job description. I had two parents that were more than capable.

Most of the time, if the help left me alone, I left them alone.

Our first maid was named Noi, meaning "little one." She was petite and pretty. She was our only maid until my youngest brother, Dan, was born. We then hired a second. Mom used to say that Noi wasn't the best at housekeeping, but she was good with baby Dan, which really turned out to be the primary responsibility for any of our house staff. This allowed Mom to work without worry. It allowed Mom and Dad to go out in the evenings and not have to find babysitters. And it gave my parents a break from the rigors of raising an infant, which turned out to be a real luxury. Not having a nanny took a bit of readjustment once we returned to the States.

Not that Mom or Dad shirked their responsibility to Dan, but when you have help that allows you to nap on occasions while raising a baby, it's huge. Mom took care of Dan at night: feedings, diaper changes, etc. Then she would get up and go to work. I have always respected my mother's work ethic.

Noi was young and beautiful. When Dan was a few months old, she left us. I thought it was for love, but Mom and I talked about this before she passed. It appeared that the maids thought I was the devil and that Mark was an angel. I call major bullshit on that. I was at least honest enough to not wear sheep's clothing. I let it all hang out. Mark could be very self-absorbed but less overt. Maybe the maids construed that as angelic. It's not that I was a jerk to anyone. I expressed how I felt. I did exhibit a temper at times. I was basically Calvin, without Hobbes to guide me.

One time a gecko, a small green lizard, was caught walking on a fresh batch of chocolate cupcakes, causing them to be thrown away. Pissed me right off, and I let everyone know it. I can understand the maids not liking that. One time I tried to kiss Noi. It didn't go well. I can understand her not liking that. I hope that wasn't the reason she left. But I assume that I could have created a little stress.

We next hired Tasani, who turned out to be the best house staffer we ever had. She was really sweet and soft spoken, but most importantly, she truly loved Dan and took really good care of him. Because of her attachment to him, though, we were worried that she would disappear with him before we left for the States a couple years later. She could easily do so, just like the gunman in the bowling alley after the murder. You worry about these things when babies are involved.

Our gardener was a college student who would pop in a day or so a week and keep the yard in shape. I don't think he ever lived with us. He may have spent the night occasionally, but he was a nice guy. I remember Mom and Dad complaining that they never saw the guy and that the yard was in a state of disrepair. Shit, I hope it wasn't me who ran him off. I mean, I surely did not try to kiss him.

The second maid hired upon Daniel's arrival was Suchin, and she proved to be the reason why background checks were such a nice thing to have. More on Suchin in a moment.

I have not written much about Dan. After all, he was a baby. What could he contribute to the conversation? At this brief moment in his life, he was cute. Of course, looks are always fleeting. I'm joking. All little brothers deserve a ration of shit now and again. But he was seriously adored. We have thousands of pictures of him from that period. I was almost twelve when Dan was born; years later, Mark and I were off to college just as Dan hit the first grade. This meant there were basically two families. There was the one that included all five of us, and as Mark and I left, there was the second. Dan was in essence an only child.

It was obvious from the beginning that Dan was a little different. He could not be in the sun without turning into a strawberry, and he choked on anything put in his mouth. I remember Dad trying to feed him mashed potatoes at the dinner table one night, and Dan just couldn't handle it. It became commonplace to see someone trying to dig food from his throat with their fingers or hanging him upside down while rapping him on the back.

Tasani's primary duties would be to help with Dan, which she loved, and Suchin would take care of the house. We thought this was a good plan, but as we learned, there was competition between the two of them. Jealousy is a dangerous thing. To sort of define Suchin as I remember her, she was a big woman, and could be very intimidating to Tasani. She was also simple and uneducated, though I don't mean to be judgmental. I always had this feeling that she was nice to our faces and then a different person when we weren't around.

One weekend, Mom and Dad left all three of us under the care of the maids; things like this were common during the 1970s. Kids were not to be seen and heard, unless they were tending bar. Today, you would end up in front of Child Protective Services for leaving a baby with the maid for three days. Mom tried to get Suchin to understand the types of baby food Dan required at different times of the day, and she struggled to write even the most basic words. You could tell she was embarrassed, and God knows what Dan ended up ingesting that weekend.

Tasani had a penchant for telling Mom and Dad the naughty goings-on of yours truly, as well as whatever things Suchin was up to. Tasani told Dad that she saw me having a smoke once, which was one of the reasons Dad had found my cigarettes. She also told them she thought Suchin was stealing from us. This is where things started to go badly.

Their relationship soured very quickly, and none of us could guess to what extent their rivalry would go. Mom and Dad were right to be concerned and started to watch for changes around the house: missing food, missing small amounts of cash, and jewelry. Evidence started to pile up to the point where Mom and Dad decided to confront Suchin.

I remember Mom and Dad sitting at the dining room table as Suchin approached. She meekly walked in, said, "Saw wat dee, ka," the basic Thai greeting of the day. Just so you know, *ka* is the effeminate and *kap* is the masculine. I would say, "Saw what dee, kap" when saying hello. Anyway, Mom and Dad returned the courtesy and asked her to sit down. You could tell Suchin was nervous.

I was not allowed to be in the room during the conversation as Mom and Dad discussed all their concerns with her. I listened to her replies to questions from atop the stairs, out of sight.

Mom and Dad tried to be very upbeat about things, and at the end, they gave Suchin a chance to redeem herself and save her job. The conversation ended quietly and respectfully. Suchin left the meeting basically on probation. What we didn't know was that she was furious, at Tasani. And Suchin was out for revenge.

One day sometime after this event, Mark and I arrived home on the school bus. As we approached the large iron gate to our driveway, there was a young man sitting on a very expensive motorcycle, a dirt bike. It was huge compared to what most Thais puttered around on. He had to be making considerable money to own this thing. We both gave him the respectful greeting of the day, and he did not return our courtesy. He just stared at us. As we passed, I noticed the man had a holster and a pistol on his belt, out for everyone to see. I asked the man if he was police, but again, he just stared at us.

Mark and I went through the gate, closing it and making sure it was locked. Immediately, we looked for anyone who was home. Neither Tasani nor Suchin were there. Odd. We went to Mom, who called Dad, who called the police. But before the cops arrived, the man had disappeared. Later that night, under the cover of darkness, Tasani returned home, shaken. There was still no sign of Suchin. Tasani told us the man was an assassin, hired by Suchin to kill her, so she had to get out of the house that day for her protection. Suchin was AWOL.

I know these stories keep getting crazier and crazier, but if you look at our lives from the moment we got to Bangkok—hot LZ in Saigon, coup d'état in the first month, murder at the bowling alley, twelve-year-old boys at whorehouses—why wouldn't having a maid who hires a hit man to take out another maid be possible? Plus, this was how this nice man on the pretty motorcycle made his money.

Our lives had gone from unique and comfortable with a smattering of craziness now and again to downright fear-for-our-lives insane. If Tasani were home that afternoon, she would have died, and what could have happened to the rest of us in the house? A killer must cover his tracks.

Suchin finally came home, and my parents confronted her. Like the first one, this conversation did not go well. In fact, it made things far worse. Tasani in short order told us that Suchin had now hired a gunman to kill us all and she had left the house. It was time for my parents to act.

Dad's first action was to brief his chain of command, including his boss, Colonel Cannon. They immediately began to discuss the issue with the Thai police, but in all honesty, no one felt the police would be effective at stopping anything from happening. We could move into the Chao Prya Hotel, but that was not a permanent solution. Another option was to put Mom, Mark, Dan, and me on an airplane and send us back to Fayetteville. That was probably the safest option, but we didn't want to leave Dad in-country alone. He would have had to finish his tour without us there. Can you imagine how hard that would be on a family and a marriage? And his life was in danger, too. Truth is, none of us wanted that.

This is when Dad called Aswan.

Rarely do common men get to see the effect of true power. Like my father, I was a career soldier, so I have seen the behavior of men who are given power by their governments or the apparatuses they serve. But in no way had I seen true power, the ability to affect a situation, create an outcome, to change a path with complete unwavering authority without having to answer or be accountable to anyone or any apparatus until that day.

Dad was very direct when he talked to Aswan. Running out of options, and possibly even time, he asked Aswan for help. Aswan calmly replied, "Have the woman available this afternoon. I will meet you at your house."

That evening, before dusk, Aswan showed up. He was dressed in his uniform and looked as sharp as ever. My parents and he exchanged niceties and discussed the situation, then Aswan asked for Suchin to come in and talk with the group.

At first Suchin was a little arrogant, until she saw who was sitting at the table. It appears that Aswan's family was well known. Aswan began the conversation. "I believe you know why we are here." Suchin said nothing.

Aswan spoke again. "Do you know who I am?" Suchin meekly nodded yes.

Aswan again. "Do you know who my father is?"

Suchin replied yes. This simple woman somehow knew of Aswan's family. It appeared that prominent and powerful military officers often appeared on television in those days, like during a coup d'état.

This is the point of the story that always makes me emotional. I can never tell it without tears. Aswan took out a loaded pistol and put it on the table. He looked sternly into Suchin's eyes and said, "This family is protected."

Suchin turned white. I have always wondered if she was just scared for her own life, or if she realized the magnitude of the statement.

"This family is protected."

If she was responsible for any of us getting hurt, to what lengths would Aswan go? Maybe imagining the possibilities was the reason for Suchin's fear.

I was listening and watching all of this from the top of the stairs. Sound traveled easily with glass walls and wooden floors, and I could watch it without exposing myself. It was dusk, so the lights were on in the dining room, and I saw what was happening at the table in the reflection of the windows that ran adjacent to the stairs.

When the conversation started, I could hardly breathe. When Aswan took out the gun, my heart stopped. Our lives were in the balance, and this was the critical moment of this ordeal.

As my father tells this story, "That witch turned white, got up and left, and never came back." Aswan saved the day. I don't think we could ever fully thank him. Also, I don't think we will ever fully understand all the nuances at play during that conversation, nor would we fully understand the concept of being "protected" in such a culture.

Was the real power of the conversation the gun, or was it something much bigger, a powerful Thai family willing to do what it takes to protect a falong family out of friendship and honor?

Dad always said that Aswan indicated there would be retribution if things went badly afterward. Dad assumed that Suchin's family would be exterminated, but that was and is an assumption.

Powerful families don't become and stay powerful by being reckless and foolish. On the other hand, Dad could be right. We saw how easily a murderer got away at the bowling alley. How hard would it be to make one or more common Thai people disappear? The truth is, we may never know, but whatever Aswan did, it worked.

We never see anyone like the motorcycle gunman again. We cautiously began to put the episode behind us, but I don't think we were ever fully comfortable on Soi Charanmit after that. Bangkok was changing for us. It was no longer beautiful and unique. Was Bangkok too wild, too lawless, and too dangerous? We began to feel it was time to go home.

CHAPTER 11

Things Change, Hard Goodbyes

Most accompanied overseas military assignments, meaning those where the entire family could come along, were normally between twenty-four and thirty-six months in length. There were also unaccompanied tours, like South Korea and Vietnam, where families could not go. These tours were usually a year. After all our trouble happened with the maids, we were at the two-year mark of a three-year tour, and we were already yearning to come home.

It's a strange and powerful emotion to be so far away from your home, feeling out of place in your current situation, and wishing it was time to hop on an outbound plane. In the Army, they call it short-timer's disease—perhaps a mild form of depression. Either way, Bangkok was losing its luster.

After the incident with the maids, we all felt differently, less settled, less safe. Our little hamlet, school, and the Rec Center didn't seem the same anymore. Mark and I could never get off the bus and rush in for a snack and a quick change of clothes without wondering who might come to the door. I am sure Mom and Dad were looking around corners, too.

I graduated from the elementary school and proceeded to junior high at ISB Bangsue. I had gone from being one of the top sixth-grade dogs to being a lowly seventh grader. I was a small fish swimming in a big pond. Everything was changing about me.

The gods of puberty were considering me, but not as kindly as they appeared to do with females. The girls seemed to simply show up at school one day with boobs. I was a smelly, sweaty weirdo. My face was oily with pimples that seemed as big as boiled eggs on my nose. There was nothing I could put on my armpits to keep them from staining my shirts, and my love stick had a mind of its own. Girls will never know how embarrassing it is to be called to work a math problem on the blackboard in class with a throbbing boner. Like Robin Williams said, "God gave man a brain and a penis, and only enough blood to work one at a time."

Happenings at the Rec Center were different, too. I was too old for Little League and now had to play in the Senior League with high school guys who were much bigger, stronger, and faster than the pubescent ogre.

In Little League, the base paths were sixty feet long. In Senior League, they used a Major League-sized field, with ninety-foot base paths. Most times at bat, I struck out from much faster pitching. If I luckily made contact with the ball, I was usually thrown out before I left the batter's box. Plus, catchers were guys who were also offensive linemen on the football team—thick with no necks. They looked like Johnny Bench making the throw to second base.

For me as a catcher, my attempt to pick off stealers on a Major League-sized field needed two bounces and a roll. Seriously, it was hard going from being the all-star catcher on the Little League winning team, hitting over .400, to being the guy who maybe got to sit in right field for two innings and have a single at bat, if I was lucky.

Things got weird at the Rec Center, too. One afternoon, an ice cream delivery guy showed up to fill the vending machines. They delivery guys were usually cool and would give us an ice cream from their freezer. This was where I first tried durian ice cream. Remember, durian is a huge fruit with creamy and sweet meat inside that literally smells like shit, but Thais love the stuff. I stuck with vanilla.

This delivery guy turned out to be a little different. That day, I was the only one who was around when he got there, so I did the normal thing and asked for a handout. He gave me one but then wanted something in return.

He got very close to me and started to touch my shoulders. I freaked out and punched him in the stomach. It didn't hurt him, so his advances turned hostile. He started smacking me on the head. I ran away as fast as I could, and he followed. I ran inside the meeting hall where there were other Americans around. Finally, he called off the attack. I can only assume what he wanted, but hands on my body scared me.

Also, next door to the Rec Center, a group of enterprising Thais began building a huge hotel-like structure. From the outside it was a beautiful building, a big change, considering that the land there used to be klong. About six months into the project, we noticed they were using parts of the building before it was finished. I am sure you can guess why. It was a giant whorehouse. We called it the Hooker Hilton. It was common for groups of drunken idiots to roam around the complex.

One day, as we walked out to the baseball diamond for practice, a bunch of drunks were sitting on top of the roof, yelling at us as we passed by. As we got a few hundred yards away, we heard a crack and something whiz by probably ten feet above our heads. Those assholes shot at us!

They were too far away to get a hit, but those drunk, lawless assholes shot at us! We did what any good Army brats would do; we ran for cover and then maneuvered off the field into a building.

I didn't hear the same sound again until combat duty in the Persian Gulf.

You never forget such incidents. Funny thing, though, we all just shrugged it off. We didn't go screaming, "Call the police!" to some adult. The police wouldn't have done a thing. Even if they had gone into the whorehouse looking for those guys, the owners would have paid them off as they got to the door, maybe given them a free turn from one of the girls. It would have been a waste of time. We just went about our day.

Was Thailand having the same effect on us that it had on all the people in the bowling alley that night?

The saddest part of being an Army brat was saying goodbye. Always being the new kid in school was never easy. Still, being the new kid in a school of fellow brats made things easier. But seeing people leave, or leaving yourself, was always heartbreaking.

In mid-1975, even the families that made up our little hamlet were leaving. First it was the Champlain family. Their big house was a little scary when empty, but it was a lot quieter. Then the Keeners moved to Japan. Finally, the Telfers had to leave unexpectedly. Mrs. Telfer developed tuberculosis, so they were moved to Walter Reed Medical Center in Washington, DC. Sadly, I heard years later, she died from the disease. Our little community was empty and sad.

The wait to make our exit seemed like it took forever. It was just no fun seeing the empty houses where we used to play and enjoy childhood. There wasn't a lot of talk about our next assignment, until one day Dad announced that he was being sent to a nine-month school in Mississippi. My reaction? *You have got to be fucking kidding me!* Even North Carolina and Georgia desegregated before Mississippi. We were going from an environment where we did not approach relationships by race to one where it was the norm. Mississippi was about as culturally opposite of Bangkok as it could be. We were not excited, to say the least.

Once moved, my worries were somewhat soothed. We moved to a beautiful area on the Gulf of Mexico. The weather was great, most of the time. Everyone liked to talk about hurricanes, but things like fishing and golf were top-notch.

The education system, after ISB, was archaic and much easier. The secret to academic success in a classroom there was to not make waves. If you were good, and White, you made at least Bs. I did next to nothing and made the honor roll every term.

I had no way to know what Mississippi life would be like, so I was uneasy. Going from one cultural extreme to another and having to cope would be a chore, but it was time to move. Movers came, packed our stuff, and soon our wonderful house was empty. Sadly, we had to give away our dog Crash, though it was to a loving family happy to have him. He would have had to sit in quarantine for months before he could get through US Customs, so we decided to find him a new home in Bangkok.

The next stop was the Chao Pyra Hotel, the same place we stayed upon our arrival. We brought Tasani with us so she could watch Dan and spend some time with him before we left.

The hotel didn't have the same luster we experienced three and a half years before. Although nothing had changed, it was still beautiful and full of life, we were tired and ready to go. I remember the time dragging on, waiting for the big day.

There were far bigger and more profound things going on in the world, though. The war in Vietnam was coming to a conclusion—one that was not positive for our Western-leaning friends and their families. As a result, the US military presence in Thailand was being reduced. Bases were closing all over the country, and basic support like commissary and PX stores were being reduced. This influenced all aspects of our lives there.

The communist takeover in Saigon made a lot of people nervous. One night before we moved out of our house, Kun and Kun Ma (Mr. and Mrs. Iyutt) came to the house and wanted to talk to Mom and Dad. Communist governments were very brutal to populations as they overthrew governments. Anyone with economic, political, or any sort of social status were executed. Millions died in this region of the world as a result, in Vietnam, Cambodia, Laos, and Burma. Intellectuals were a common target. Kun and Kun Ma Iyutt were Cornell-trained medical doctors.

The conversation that night revolved around the fear over

Thailand's path. Would it be civil war, a communist takeover, and then mass exterminations? What the Iyutts asked for wasn't to save their own hides; they asked whether we would take their daughter back to the States with us, and care for her if the worst happened.

Of course, my parents agreed. I remember the poor girl sitting there, listening to the conversation. It was incredibly apparent from her face that she wanted nothing to do with this. If she left, she would never see her parents again. How horrible. And to live with a strange family, in a foreign country. How sad? Think about it; her parents were Ivy League—educated doctors. She lived in a high socio-economic culture. We would have surely been a step down. But the deal was made.

Thankfully, the strong Thai monarchy and their superb military never allowed this to happen. Thailand, to this day, remains the only country in Southeast Asia that never slipped into communism. We had other friends, however, whose loyalty to country had a much more dramatic effect. Tommy and Tino Chao were two schoolmates from South Vietnam. Their father worked at the South Vietnamese embassy in Bangkok. They were nice guys, and I considered them friends. Tommy was tall and slim, always friendly and laughing. Tino was shorter and stocky. He was more serious, not as fun loving as his brother, and really good at Tae Kwon Do, which I learned the hard way. We were all in Boy Scouts, so we camped and went to Pattaya Scout Camp together. They were also on the River Quai and Arawan Falls trips.

As Saigon fell, the new government closed all its embassies. No sovereign Western-centric country would recognize a communist government. The new regime, now in the newly named Ho Chi Minh City, ordered all diplomats home. The Chaos felt a duty to return.

I have often wondered what happened to Tommy and Tino. I hope they are okay. Every time I think of Bangkok, I remember them.

Our big day finally arrived. We got up, made sure all of our bags were packed for travel, and all went out the same door we had entered our first day in-country, three and a half years earlier. This time, we left the air-conditioned comfort and walked into tropical heat for the last time. Major Richardson showed up, probably with the same van, loaded us up, and moved carefully into traffic. Tasani came with us.

The superhighway was in full parade. As we passed by ISB Bangsue, we all took a final look. When we arrived at the airport, Major Richardson parked the van and came into the terminal to say goodbye.

You can't overstate the importance of good friends, especially in circumstances like Thailand, and the Richardson family were good and loyal friends. My dad still keeps in touch with them.

As we sat next to the airplane, waiting to board, we all kept an eye on Tasani and Dan. Dan was in a stroller, and Tasani was moving him about. There was no reason to be concerned. Tasani was a good woman and a loyal and trustworthy caregiver to Dan. I prayed that the remainder of her life would be filled with love, happiness, and joy.

As the airline called us to board, we all said our goodbyes. Tasani cried as she hugged Dan for the last time. It always breaks my heart to think of that. As she said goodbye to us, Dad gave her a large sum of money, and she disappeared into the crowd.

Handshakes and hugs were given to Major Richardson, and we were off. The aircraft door closed, and a few moments later, we had our last glimpses of Thailand.

CHAPTER 12

The Long Road Home

Our first stop was Hong Kong, and the plan was to spend the night there. Just a few hours from Bangkok by air, it was a completely new world—cold, rainy, and foggy. We had not seen fog in three-plus years, nor had we needed additional layers of clothing, much less long pants. After landing, we took a taxi to our hotel and settled in.

Hong Kong at the time was still British. We turned on the TV, and the BBC was on. I got to see a music show that played videos. This was amazing. Television in Bangkok was in its infancy, and most programming was in Thai.

The first video was Elton John playing "Crocodile Rock" live with his great band. The album *Goodbye Yellow Brick Road* was popular then and selling like crazy in Bangkok. We had heard and memorized almost all the songs. The video was a real treat. We also got to see many British bands on the show: Rod Stewart, the Stones, and members of the Beatles who were now making music independently. It was my first lesson on how ethnocentric the Brits can be. Only British acts were on this show, and I didn't understand why.

The hotel was surely more Western, more British. The carpets were royal blue, and the beds were properly made with beautiful bedspreads. We went to dinner at the restaurant on the top floor of the hotel. The view of the city, even damp and foggy, was beautiful.

As we walked out of the restaurant, two very large Chinese men entered. Have you ever met someone who made the hair on the back of your neck stand up? Everyone around tensed up. Dad said they were surely gangsters. They were dressed in black suits with black, full-length coats, plenty of area to hide a gun. We got away from them fast. Maybe our Bangkok radar was still active.

The next day we went shopping. Prices then were extremely cheap. Mark and I got new Puma sneakers for $100 Hong Kong, about $20 US. I used to fuck with the locals in Mississippi, telling them that these were Chinese Converse and they cost a hundred bucks—a ton of money then. They were so limited in scope they believed me.

Our next stop was a six-hour layover in Tokyo, which I barely remember. I do recall lugging a heavy diaper bag full of Dan's stuff, and the strap of the bag dug into my shoulder as we went from one gate to another.

The next hop would put us on US soil for the first time since 1972. It was a nine-hour trip from Tokyo to Seattle. This was the flight of Dan's great caca catastrophe.

Although Dan was much younger and a bit coddled, he was not spared from the wrath of his big brothers. Dan will always be the guy who makes the untimely faux pas that will go down in the history books as hysterically funny, at least to his older brothers. His first major performance was on the flight from Tokyo to Seattle.

Still in diapers, he took a dump so large that it filled his diaper way beyond capacity and then ran up his back and into his hair. Dad, not knowing the extent of the dump, smelled something and went for a blind diaper check. As he pulled his hand away, it was covered in the great caca. Dan just lay there looking relieved with a contented smirk.

Mom and Dad resorted to putting liquid Benadryl in his bottle to sedate him on flights and hopefully keep his bowels under control. I wonder what the other people in this flying tube thought for the remainder of our ten-hour flight. I am sure they had to sterilize the aircraft afterward.

When we landed in Seattle, it was freezing. We got home in the early fall of 1975, so the weather had turned in the Pacific Northwest. Truth was, anywhere was cold compared to Bangkok, and we were dressed in our best Nanook of the North clothing—just jeans, shoes and socks, and a sweatshirt. Funny thing, there was family in Seattle that had just traveled into town from Alaska. They were enjoying the heat wave. We were shivering, and their barefoot baby was sitting in a stroller wearing only a diaper.

The next stop was Atlanta. It was so odd being in a space with only English speakers. Everything was so . . . American. You could read the signs and have a conversation with a flight attendant without having to use your broken Thai, or any of your trustworthy cuss words. I asked a beautiful flight attendant for a 7-Up. She looked at me and said, "I'll bring you milk." Since my embarrassing show in Patpong, I was learning which sex was in charge and to fall into formation, like a good soldier.

Landing in Atlanta was a quick turnaround. We hopped on a Piedmont Airlines flight for the final ride home, to Fayetteville and Amma. We were all excited and nervous. I can still feel the butterflies in my stomach, knowing that she was so close. We had not seen Amma since moving overseas. Our only contact came from the occasional phone call and letter. Mom and Dad had offered to fly her to Bangkok, but she never agreed.

As we took off, Mom was already crying. In an hour, our journey would come full circle.

As the wheels touched down in Fayetteville, you could feel the excitement and emotion building between all of us. I struggled to get a glimpse of Amma through the airplane window. We all knew she was in the terminal and waiting for us. We could not get off the airplane fast enough.

We walked as fast as we could off the jetway. Mom and Dad kept telling us to slow down. They had a baby and a stroller to tend to, but we could not contain ourselves. We turned the corner into the terminal and then, she was there.

From that moment on it was an outpouring of emotion. We ran to Amma's arms, as she crying uncontrollably. Then Mom and Dad, with Dan, joined us. It had been three years. She looked older, tired. I am not sure if happy was the emotion we all felt. I think it was more like relief. So much had changed. None of us were the same. There was so much to share and to learn, like we had to reintroduce ourselves.

Amma brought a friend with her to airport, her next-door neighbor Ms. Baker, so we had a couple of cars to get us home. Driving through Fayetteville seemed very different. There were new businesses and buildings everywhere, so much I didn't recognize. Where was my Fayetteville?

Getting home and going into the house was like walking into the past. Amma's house had not changed. Other than her starting to collect commemorative plates and hang them on the wall, everything was the same. Of course, the first thing she wanted to do was feed us. She asked me what I wanted, and I said, "A peanut butter sandwich and a glass of milk." These were things we didn't see often at the commissary in Bangkok, and if they were there, they had survived ocean voyages in containers, and sat at ports in the hot sun, so the freshness was gone. Bread in Bangkok was like eating hardtack at times, and peanut butter was the consistency and taste of Play-Doh.

I took my sandwich and milk and went in the living room. I sat down a few feet from her console TV and took a bite of my sandwich. The bread seemed like it had just come out of the oven, and the peanut butter was perfectly creamy and delicious. I took a sip of milk, which was cold and fresh. I reached over to turn on the TV, and a show came on. There was 1950s music playing, and on the screen was a guy in a leather jacket and a ducktail haircut, riding a motorcycle. Little did I know, this was the show *Happy Days*, and it was hugely popular. In that perfect moment, as I enjoyed my sandwich, we were home. The next chapter of our lives was soon to begin.

EPILOGUE

Over the years, I have not kept in touch with friends from Bangkok. I went to two schools in Europe that both have strong alumni pages on Facebook, with almost daily updates on each page. For some reason, ISB has a pretty feeble page. Maybe it's because most of the American population left country as the Vietnam War ended. ISB now seems to be just a small ex-pat school. I have not been able to run down people like Mike Wright or Chris Williams. Both are common names, making them hard to search. I did try and look for Mike's father's restaurant, the Cock and Bull, with no success. There is a Pop Shop in Bangkok, but it's a toy store.

As I write this book, I have begun following several YouTuber ex-pats in Thailand. Some of the channels are really good, so I watch frequently. It's amazing to see how much Bangkok and other parts of the country have grown. My wife, Cheryl, and I have decided to go to either Chiang Mai or Koh Samui for few months after we retire in a few years. Bangkok is too big now, so we are opting for more peaceful areas of the country.

Thailand will always have a special place in my heart. I will return one day.

As I indicated often, my brother Dan is the baby in the family. He has given us a few scares throughout the years. When he was maybe three, his body stopped making white blood cells, and we braced for his passing. It was a horrible time.

Dad would secretly cry in the shower, he recently told me. One time, he was on TDY (temporary travel), so I went to a doctor's appointment for Dan with Mom. We were stationed at Fort Monroe, Virginia, at the time. During the medical appointment at the local Navy hospital, she got the news of his condition. Doctors said they needed to do additional tests, and asked if they could do a spinal tap that day. Mom was devastated and struggled to stay on her feet, so the doctor asked me to help during the procedure.

We placed Dan on a table in the doctor's office, facedown. Already he was crying, scared. The doctors asked us to take control of his limbs and hold him down, scaring him more.

Mom couldn't do it, so I held both of Dan's legs down. A Navy corpsman joined us and controlled his arms. Then the doctor took a very large-gauge needle and approached Dan.

A spinal tap is normally performed to rule out the possibility of infection, like meningitis and encephalitis. It can also help diagnose issues with the central nervous system. I don't remember exactly why this was being done, but it was terrifying to all of us when we saw the needle.

I still remember the sound of the needle piercing Dan's spine, a loud crunch as it opened a hole in the bone. It was so forceful, you could feel the penetration reverberate through his body. He screamed in terror.

Thank God the doctor extracted enough spinal fluid in a second or two. When the needle was out, Mom immediately grabbed Dan and wept while she held him. I think it was somewhat traumatizing for all of us, but I have always been able to maintain my composure when the world around me is crumbling.

I didn't cry at the doctor's office. I cried later at my friend's house, a good man named Bob Faller. We got home to our quarters on Fort Monroe, and I immediately hopped on my skateboard and pushed toward Bob's. I walked into his house, sat down at their dining room table, and just fell apart. I have always been grateful that they allowed me to do that.

Dad tells this story about praying over Dan in his bed at night during this period. One night while he knelt over Dan, a voice clearly said to him, "He's okay." Dad thought someone else was in the room. He checked me and Mark, but we were asleep. He looked under the bed and in the closet. There was no one. We are all convinced it was Dan's guardian angel looking over him. And as the angel said, Dan would recover and be all right. We have all taken our place in protecting Dan. He has always needed it.

Today, he and his wife live at the Jersey Shore. They have four beautiful children and live about ten minutes from my dad. Having Dan live close to Dad after Mom passed was a godsend for both of them.

After Dan recovered from his medical issues earlier in life, he struggled a bit with school. But he made up for his academic deficiency with hard work and loyalty. Of course, we don't know if his medical issues contributed. He always worked as hard as he could to finish college, but it just didn't happen. It was hardest on Dad. He is a good man, a loving husband, and an amazing father. But Dan would do anything to help a friend. He is an honorable man, and I am proud that he is my brother.

Mark met the love of his life at a Sigma Phi Epsilon/Lambda Chi Alpha party at NC State, in 1984. They have been together since, and live outside of Raleigh, NC. After graduating from NC State, he was commissioned in the US Marine Corps and stationed at Camp Lejeune. At the end of his initial tour, he decided to get out and move the family back to Raleigh, where they raised three amazing kids—two boys and a girl. Mark now works for the Environmental Protection Agency and is a retired Marine Corps Reserve officer.

Mark is one of the most spiritual people I have ever known, and he has an ability to always see a peaceful path for any situation. It is a trait I lack. But, like Dan, he is an honorable man. He has always been a faithful and loving husband, and truly a dedicated father. I admire him tremendously.

My mom and dad were the best of friends. Mom passed in August of 2018. Dad is an extremely passionate man, and his love for her taught the men in his family how to treat a woman, a wife, a mother. When Mom contracted cancer for a second time early in that year, Dad did everything he could to save her. He made sure she got to the best cancer center in the country, Memorial Sloan Ketterling in New York. After doctors ran out of options, we brought her home, and Dad took care of her around the clock for five months. I am so proud of how he stepped up to the plate for her.

The night she passed, I was home in Harrisburg. Around 3 p.m. he rang and was panicking. She had been teetering for weeks, but she had surely moved into the final stage before death. I got on the road a couple hours later, and finally got to them around 9 p.m. that night.

Mom was incoherent and struggling to breathe. We all sat together until around midnight, and Dad suggested I go up and try to sleep. I agreed, and as I did, I told Mom it was okay to go. I kissed her on her forehead and went upstairs.

Dad turned out the lights and dozed on the couch next to her hospital bed, which was in the living room. A couple hours later, something woke me up, and then a couple minutes later, Dad called for me. I rushed downstairs, and she was gone. I guess she just wanted to pass on her own time, alone. Maybe she didn't want me to see her go.

Cancer had devoured her. The last time I saw her face, the coroner was covering her in a blanket and rolling her out of the house on a gurney. That image is burned in my mind.

I have never seen anyone in more pain than Dad. Grief consumed him, and when it happened, I thought he would never fully recover. But I will say, after some time, he has made peace with Mom's passing and has stood up for himself, determined to have happiness and joy in the remainder of his life. This is the sign of true strength and one that makes me truly proud of him. He now bides his time doing what he loves—reading, and reaching out to his fellow paratrooper friends, and he does so much for Dan's kids. He spends a lot of time with them, and they adore him for it. It's what Mom would have wanted him to do.

Thankfully, Dan and his family are close. With Mark living in North Carolina and me living in Pennsylvania, it's good to know Dan can get to him if needed.

I have to be honest, it was hard for me seeing the man who was the strength in our family destroyed by the loss of my mother. After all, from the time he drove up to Amma's house that day in 1971, he was the man who protected us. He and I went through some hard times after Mom left, two type-A personalities battling over ridiculous issues. It was just grief.

Happily, we have worked through our issues, and thank God Mark's logical manner was there to help us focus on what was truly important. I wrote this book to find the memory of the warrior he once was and still is, to feel close to him again. My respect and gratitude for him is greater than ever.

As for me, life has seen its ups and downs. Life after Bangkok led me to many places in the US, as well as life in Europe. After graduating from high school in Belgium, I floundered through my undergraduate years, in fraternity houses and keg parties. I am proud to say, though, I had the opportunity to attend the University of Maryland, Munich Campus. It was a small school, in an amazing city, for military kids living in Europe. It beat the hell out of moving back to the States, and had a similar atmosphere as life in Bangkok, especially in terms of race and culture. If you haven't noticed, my behavior can be a bit erratic at times, so after leaving Munich, I squandered an ROTC scholarship at NC State. Munich was a two-year school. I ended up at a mediocre college in northern New Jersey to finally finish my bachelor's degree. It was a fun school. From my dorm window, on a clear day, you could see every skyscraper in the Manhattan skyline.

School was never hard for me. It bored me. It was a means to an end. I remember that when we returned from Thailand to

Mississippi, schooling there was almost a joke. My lack of discipline finally caught up to me in high school.

After having three junior years in college, I graduated by the skin of my teeth. Luckily, and with Dad's help, I was allowed to attend the Officer Candidate School at Fort Benning, to finally achieve something in my immature life.

I needed the structure that the Army provided, but more importantly, I wanted a mechanism that would allow me to live in the magnificent places of my youth, like Bangkok, Belgium, and then West Germany.

After completing Basic Training at Fort Knox, Officer Candidate School at Fort Benning, and the host of schools that lieutenants get to attend to prepare them for their first assignment, I went to Airborne School, and had a course about my beloved Bradley Infantry Fighting vehicle. The Army in Europe was heavy, meaning armored, all designed to resist Russian armored formations. Thank God we never clashed with the Russians.

In November of 1988, I left for Friedberg, Germany, and 1st Battalion, 36th Infantry, 3rd Brigade, 3rd Armored Division. Spearhead. It was the same place Elvis was stationed in the 1950s. Being a young officer in an infantry battalion was truly hard. The hours were brutal, the physical environment the same, and my job was to train thirty soldiers to raise a rifle to their eye and pull the trigger. If you have ever really thought about the concept, it can be horrifying. Constant training and indoctrination makes the idea of killing someone acceptable. It's something that I struggle with today, because eventually we got our opportunity to apply our trade. We were one of the parade of units that deployed to the first Gulf War. We were really lucky to outclass our enemy. No army on the planet could defeat a great American armored formation. That's why our enemies today take the fight elsewhere.

I married after the first tour in Europe, just after the Persian Gulf War. My first wife was not suited for the life of a warrior's wife, though. It's sad to say, but I married outside my culture. I was an Army brat who saw many different variations of the human condition. She was a beautiful Italian girl from Essex County, New Jersey, who grew up without a care in the world. That's not a criticism, but the truth. Why she married me I will never understand. Maybe it was the romance of a soldier returning from war.

Places like Fort Bragg were just too lonely for her. To be fair, we did have some tough times. Due to illness, my military career ended early, and I took work as a Department of the Army civilian. We opened a bookstore with at one time the largest collection of aviation books on the planet. For a time, the store did well, but when the market crashed in the late 2000s, the business failed, and it was just too much for her. I guess I let her down too many times. I just wasn't what she needed, and in 2007, she asked for a divorce.

I regret so many of my mistakes. I never wanted a divorce, but in the end, it was what she wanted, so I agreed. Determined to not let my children down like my biological father had, we held off on divorce until 2014. There were many hard years, and I was devastated, but I was not going to walk away from my kids. They had to be okay before we divorced.

My ex and I have five beautiful, bright children. I know I may be a little biased, but it's true. My oldest son, Luke, taught himself Japanese, including writing. After graduating from college, he went to Japan to teach English to young children. After a year on a remote Japanese island, dying of boredom, he opted to return home and settle in Seattle. He worked for a couple years as a freelance artist and college professor but now has taken his place in the economy, working for a major Japanese company. When he got the job, he called me and said, "They are paying me a ridiculous amount of money." You have to understand, working for the "man" was a sin just a couple days earlier.

My oldest daughter, Emily, lives in Virginia with her husband and my two beautiful granddaughters. The divorce was hardest on her. It was so hard to watch, and I felt so much guilt. She had to blame someone, so I was her logical target. For years, I felt helpless. We sent her to Richmond for college. She rebelled, kind of like me. But she doesn't take shit from anyone and is a strong mother, wife, and woman. She's finishing her degree at Virginia Commonwealth and is doing magnificently. I fought for years to mend our relationship. Finally, my effort paid off. We have a great respect and love for one another now. My little punker girl has grown up.

Twin sons Noah and Jacob have both completed their studies. Noah is in Atlanta, trying to get a foothold in the music or television industries. It's amazing how many scumbags there are in those businesses. But he's tough, and I am amazed at his work ethic and proud of him. His twin, Jake, is beginning a career as a sound engineer. COVID has made it hard on him, but he will get back on his feet. He is smart and charming.

Then there is Olivia. Born just a few years before my first wife asked for a divorce, she became my constant companion. I was her strength, and she was mine. For a time, we were inseparable. My baby. She, like all her siblings, is very creative. She goes to a local magnet school and studies art. She's good at it.

Then there is my wonderful stepdaughter, Abby, who also struggled with our divorce. She is so bright, beautiful, and strong. She's at university now and is doing amazing things. She wants to join the Foreign Service or Peace Corps. She makes me proud.

It took some time for us to develop a relationship. Like Emily, she was angry and hurt. I was the logical bad guy, trying to take her mother away. It took some time for her see that wasn't true. We now have a great relationship. As with Emily, if it's important, you never give up.

Abby is fluent in French. After high school, she went to Belgium for a year to hone her craft. I told her as she left, "Once you go there, your soul will always want to return." She sees and feels that now, just like I feel for Thailand.

In 2014, I met the love of my life. After my long separation and divorce, I was done with women, but I realized that God brought Cheryl and I together so we could fix our lives and be happy together. My wife is the most kind and loving person I have ever known. She must be my guardian angel. I surely could not have gotten it together without her. We are equals. She is my Ezer, a Biblical reference. I am her Ezer. Now all we want to do is spend the rest of our lives together and return to Europe and my beloved Thailand one day.

CPSIA information can be obtained
at www.ICGtesting.com
Printed in the USA
BVHW032322140223
658501BV00004B/117